Financial Advisor Series

ETHICS FOR THE FINANCIAL SERVICES PROFESSIONAL
PROFESSIONAL
Fourth Edition

Julie Anne Ragatz
Ronald F. Duska

THE
AMERICAN
COLLEGE PRESS

FA290.04.1

This publication is designed to provide accurate and authoritative information about the subject covered. While every precaution has been taken in the preparation of this material, the authors, and The American College assume no liability for damages resulting from the use of the information contained in this publication. The American College is not engaged in rendering legal, accounting, or other professional advice. If legal or other expert advice is required, the services of an appropriate professional should be sought.

© 2010 The American College Press
270 S. Bryn Mawr Avenue
Bryn Mawr, PA 19010
(888) AMERCOL (263-7265)
theamericancollege.edu
All rights reserved
Library of Congress Control Number 2010910507
ISBN-10: 1-58293-038-4
ISBN-13: 978-1-58293-038-1
Printed in the United States of America

Sales Skills Techniques

Techniques for Exploring Personal Markets

Techniques for Meeting Client Needs

Techniques for Prospecting: Prospect or Perish

Marketing Financial Services to Women

Product Essentials

Essentials of Annuities

Essentials of Business Insurance

Essentials of Disability Income Insurance

Essentials of Life Insurance Products

Essentials of Long-Term Care Insurance

Essentials of Multiline Insurance Products

Planning Foundations

Foundations of Estate Planning

Foundations of Financial Planning: An Overview

Foundations of Financial Planning: The Process

Foundations of Investment Planning

Foundations of Retirement Planning

The American College® is an independent, nonprofit, accredited institution founded in 1927 that offers professional certification and graduate-degree distance education to men and women seeking career growth in financial services.

The Center for Financial Advisor Education at The American College offers both the LUTCF and the Financial Services Specialist (FSS) professional designations to introduce students in a classroom environment to the technical side of financial services, while at the same time providing them with the requisite sales-training skills.

The Solomon S. Huebner School® of The American College administers the Chartered Life Underwriter (CLU®); the Chartered Financial Consultant (ChFC®); the Chartered Advisor for Senior Living (CASL®); the Registered Health Underwriter (RHU®); the Registered Employee Benefits Consultant (REBC®); and the Chartered Leadership Fellow®(CLF®) professional designation programs. In addition, the Huebner School also administers The College's CFP Board—registered education program for those individuals interested in pursuing CFP® certification, the CFP® Certification Curriculum.

The Richard D. Irwin Graduate School® of The American College offers the master of science in financial services (MSFS) degree, the Graduate Financial Planning Track (another CFP Board-registered education program), and several graduate-level certificates that concentrate on specific subject areas. It also offers the Chartered Advisor in Philanthropy (CAP®) and the master of science in management (MSM), a one-year program with an emphasis in leadership. The National Association of Estate Planners & Councils has named The College as the provider of the education required to earn its prestigious AEP designation.

The American College is accredited by **The Middle States Commission on Higher Education**, 3624 Market Street, Philadelphia, PA 19104 at telephone number 267.284.5000.

The Middle States Commission on Higher Education is a regional accrediting agency recognized by the U.S. Secretary of Education and the Commission on Recognition of Postsecondary Accreditation. Middle States accreditation is an expression of confidence in an institution's mission and goals, performance, and resources. It attests that in the judgment of the Commission on Higher Education, based on the results of an internal institutional self-study and an evaluation by a team of outside peer observers assigned by the Commission, an institution is guided by well-defined and appropriate goals; that it has established conditions and procedures under which its goals can be realized; that it is accomplishing them substantially; that it is so organized, staffed, and supported that it can be expected to continue to do so; and that it meets the standards of the Middle States Association. The American College has been accredited since 1978.

The American College does not discriminate on the basis of race, religion, sex, handicap, or national and ethnic origin in its admissions policies, educational programs and activities, or employment policies.

The American College is located at 270 S. Bryn Mawr Avenue, Bryn Mawr, PA 19010. The toll-free number of the Office of Professional Education is (888) AMERCOL (263-7265); the fax number is (610) 526-1465; and the home page address is theamericancollege.edu.

CONTENTS

In the last decade of the 20th century, the landscape in the financial services industry began to change rapidly. For more than 50 years, financial services were segmented. This was a direct result of legislation passed during the Great Depression of the 1930s. Banks could not sell insurance and insurance companies sold only insurance. The invention of new financial instruments, such as mutual funds and retirement funds; the increase in longevity, which made long-term care and retirement funds as important as, if not more important than life insurance; and the passage of the Financial Services Modernization Act (Gramm-Leach-Bliley) caused the development of new distribution systems. One-stop shopping became a possibility in financial markets. No longer did one need to go to an insurance agent for insurance, a bank for a loan, and a mutual fund salesperson for different investments. Financial planners began to look over clients' entire portfolios and recommend a variety of instruments and products, a balance of which best fit the now more complex needs of those clients.

Though extremely useful in the past, books such as *Piecing Together the Ethical Puzzle* and *Charting an Ethical Course*, which were created to instruct newly minted insurance salespeople in the ethics of insurance sales, needed to be modified and expanded to meet current-day realities.

Hence, this book addresses the basic ethical issues the financial services professional needs to be cognizant of today. While ethics that governs the scale of insurance is an important element in the picture, there are now other elements that are equally as important that govern the sales of other financial instruments.

Still, there is commonality to all of these products—they are used to help facilitate financial risk management and they have the benefit of removing the anxiety that might come from a client's lack of financial security. *Securities* are aptly named. They can create security for people and the freedom from worry, as does insurance. One cannot remove all anxiety and uncertainty from life, but by helping a client develop a well-balanced portfolio, a financial services professional can help produce benefits for clients that were undreamed of in the past, such as a degree of freedom from financial anxiety.

This is the noble goal of the financial services professional who, in his or her own way, is as important to the client as the client's doctor or lawyer. One of the conditions of happiness, according to the ancient Greek philosopher, Aristotle, is to have enough wealth so one's existence is not continually beset by financial worry. How a financial services professional can effect that laudable goal in an ethical manner is the subject of this book.

To acclimate to the changing realities, we will treat some subjects in a general way, such as the nature of ethics and the ethical responsibilities of being a professional, and the relationship between law and ethics. But we will also delve further into other more specific practices, such as what is ethically necessary in the sale of insurance as opposed to what is ethically necessary in the sale of securities.

The field of financial services is filled with a bewildering array of things to learn, ranging from sophisticated products to sales techniques. Perhaps, though, the most important thing to learn is how to do one's job in an ethical manner with integrity. How should I treat my employer, the companies I represent, my fellow financial services professionals and, most of all, my clients?

To paraphrase Shakespeare, we think being ethical makes you "twice blest." You are blessed because, as we will show, being ethical goes with having a *noble* purpose in life, which is essential for one to flourish as a human being and to fill life with immense satisfaction—a satisfaction money cannot buy. Secondly, being ethical also helps you stay out of trouble while gaining you a good reputation. Good ethics is good business.

Thus, our firm conviction is that for financial services professionals ethics is beneficial on both personal and financial levels.

ACKNOWLEDGMENTS

This book and its accompanying course is the result of taking the best of two LUTC ethics books, *Piecing Together the Ethical Puzzle* and *Charting an Ethical Course*, along with part of The American College book, *The Regulation of the Life Insurance Business* by Jon S. Hanson, melding their content together, thoroughly revising that content, and adding a substantial amount of new material. We gratefully acknowledge the generosity of innumerable organizations and individuals who assisted in developing those courses with their advice, suggestions, and/or contributions of material.

Such a book is not possible without the joint effort of numerous people. I would like to thank them for what is worthwhile about the book, while holding none of them responsible for any of its shortcomings.

Specifically, I owe a great debt of gratitude to the following people at The American College. Samuel H. Weese, former President and CEO, who encouraged The American College's original production of this book and course of study for LUTC candidates. Larry Barton, President and CEO for his constant encouragement, as well as Walt Woerheide, Vice President for Academic Affairs for his support. Special thanks for those who's contribution could not be overlooked: Edward E. Graves, Associate Professor of Insurance, who helped by checking the manuscript for fidelity to existing regulations and procedures in the financial services marketplace; Jane Hassinger, for her keen eye for detail; Patricia Cheers, for her outstanding ability to secure permissions; Todd Denton, for all his editing skills; and, as always, Joe Brennan, who designed the striking cover.

My final thanks go to all the students of the past several years who, in the classes I teach at The American College, have furnished me with untold numbers of ethical situations in the financial services industry along with wise solutions to any number of those situations. I have learned much from them.

Ron Duska

Self-Study

This course is intended to be a self-contained, self-study course. That is, you should be able to complete the course and pass the test without any additional material. Although the chapters can stand alone, considerable thought has been given to their placement. The learning process will be most effective if you read and study each chapter in the order presented.

Chapter Review Quizzes

There is a short quiz at the end of each chapter. The multiple-choice questions cover material you will find on the final exam. The answers are located in the Appendix. The quiz is an excellent method to check your mastery of the material in the chapter. If you answer a quiz question incorrectly, it is best to go back and review the appropriate material immediately. You should be comfortable with the current material before moving on to the next chapter.

Final Exam and Procedure

The final exam is made up of 50 multiple-choice questions. The exam questions are similar to the multiple-choice questions in the chapter quiz sections. All the information you need concerning the exam is contained in the final exam packet to this course.

Final Exam Procedure—The final examination is administered online. To receive CE credit for this self-study course, you must pass the course examination.

The American College requires that a disinterested third party over the age of 18 proctor the final course exam. The student is responsible to ensure that the proctor complies with the state's specific requirements for proctoring a final exam.

Information regarding proctor approval and access to the final examination will be provided as part of the course confirmation immediately after your course registration is received.

You have 6 months from the date of the course registration to take the final examination. Questions regarding the exam should be addressed to Professional

Education Services at 877-655-5882.

Study Hints and Suggestions

Has it been a long time since you have taken a self-study course? Maybe this is your first experience with this method of learning. Several techniques have been developed to improve the results in a self-study environment. They have proven to be extremely effective and are worth your consideration.

Set a Goal for Completion—Set a target date for completing your studies. Do not try to do too much at once. Many people set a goal of one or two chapters per week. Put your goal in writing and post it in a prominent place.

Schedule the Time You Need—Block out the necessary time in your planner or appointment book. Consider this time as important as a sales call and resist changing it.

Study When You Are Fresh—Pick study times that occur when you are well rested and at your peak. This will maximize your retention of the material.

No Distractions—Find a quiet place to work where you are able to minimize interruptions. Try not to allow telephone, coworkers, or children to disturb you.

Highlight—Use a highlighter to emphasize important points in the text. This can improve your retention and facilitate your review for the final exam.

Review: Take the Chapter Quizzes—Take each chapter quiz and, if you have incorrect answers, review the appropriate material immediately. Record your answers on a blank piece of paper. This will allow you to take the quiz again.

Implement Ideas—The text is full of ideas that can enhance your practice while limiting malpractice liability. However, you have to use the ideas to reap the benefits.

Exercises—The text contains short exercises within each chapter. Complete these exercises during your reading. If you attend a seminar, be prepared to discuss your answers during classroom training. (Note: You will not be responsible for the information contained in the exercises for the final examination.)

ETHICS IN FINANCIAL SERVICES

What Is the Financial Services Industry?

The current shape of the financial industry reveals the linkages forged by the integration which took place in the 1980s and 1990s. Generally, the financial services industry is considered to consist of four groups, each with its own subdivisions. Broadly speaking, the financial services industry originates, distributes, services and funds financial products.

Segments of the Financial Services Industry
• Securities: Brokerage, Investment Banking
• Asset Management: Retail and Private clients, Institutional
• Commercial Banking: Retail, Wholesale
• Insurance: Life, Non-Life

Merton and Bodie claim that there are six basic functions that are required of any well-functioning financial system:[1]

1. pooling resources and subdividing shares
2. transferring resources across space and time
3. providing mechanisms to manage risk
4. providing information, especially prices, needed to coordinate decentralized decision making in the economy
5. providing mechanisms to solve the problem of asymmetric information, agency problems and incentives
6. clearing and settling payments

The products and services financial services professionals provide continue to evolve to meet the demands of individual and institutional consumers. Financial services firms and practitioners can be divided into two classes; financial intermediaries and financial facilitators. Financial intermediaries are firms that hold financial assets (such as loans, mortgages, bonds and equity securities) and issue liabilities on themselves in various forms (such as deposits, pension obligations and mutual fund shares). Financial facilitators expedite the transactions between the holders of the liabilities and those who purchase the liabilities as investments. Both intermediaries and facilitators, financial services institutions and practitioners play an essential role in both the efficient functioning of financial markets and in the financial health of market participants.[2]

Who Is the Financial Services Professional?

For the purposes of this text, financial service professionals are individuals who work within any of the industries presented in the table above. While the precise differences between professionals and salespersons will be discussed in a later chapter, because the title of this text is *Ethics for the Financial Services Professional,* the assumption is that students enrolled in this program are to willing assume the mantle of professionalism and the additional moral obligations which accompany it. According to Solomon Huebner, the founder of The American College, professionals

---

1. Erik Sirri. (2004) "Investment Banks, Scope and Unavoidable Conflicts of Interest." *Economic Review: Federal Reserve Bank of Atlanta:* 24.

2. Lawrence J. White. (1996) "Technological Change, Financial Innovation, and Financial Regulation: The Challenges for Public Policy." *Wharton Center for Financial Institutions Working Paper 97-35:* 1.

are distinguished from salespersons and other practitioners by four characteristics:

1. practicing a useful vocation
2. practicing a vocation that involves a science
3. abandoning a strictly selfish commercial point of view and keeping in mind the advantage of the client
4. maintaining a spirit of loyalty toward other professionals

In addition to a shared set of professional duties and obligations, financial services professionals are required to submit to various forms of regulation. These regulatory frameworks frequently contain specific requirements regarding the level of care which the financial services professional owes his or her client. For example, Registered Investment Advisers (RIAs), are required by law to act as a fiduciary, while other professionals are not so obliged.

Educational institutions, trade groups and self-regulatory organizations impose additional ethical duties on their members. One of the common obligations of each these groups in the financial services industry is the obligation to conduct oneself as a professional.

THE CHANGING FACE OF THE FINANCIAL SERVICES INDUSTRY

Increased Consolidation and Expansion of Financial Firms

The financial services industry has changed to meet the needs of an evolving population and economic environment. One changes in recent decades has been the tremendous growth of the financial markets. Both in terms of breadth and depth, financial markets have expanded to meet the needs of increasingly global and technologically sophisticated consumers. In terms of breadth, markets have grown in size by virtually every standard of measurement. In terms of depth, recent years have seen an incredible period of innovation resulting in a variety of new financial products, such as securitized assets (mortgage backed securities) and derivative instruments.[3] New exchanges have emerged, specializing in these financial products and have grown to become major markets.

---

3.   Franklin Allen and Anthony M. Santomero. (1996) "The Theory of Financial Intermediation." Wharton Center for Financial Institutions Working Papers 96-32: 4.

The evolving nature of financial instruments affected the structure and type of firms who operate in financial markets. In the early part of the 20th century, traditional institutions, such as banks and insurance companies, transferred the deposits and premium payments left in their care to corporations by offering loans or investing in the securities market.[4] By the 1970s and 1980s, markets changed significantly with the introduction of new financial instruments such as derivatives, as well the development of new markets for the exchange of various financial futures and options. This led to the decline of the traditional banking and insurance companies relative to other financial services firms.[5] Banks and insurance companies have responded by broadening the services they provide to consumers.

The expansion of single service providers into other lines of business was not motivated solely by increased competition. The practice of the financial services emerged as an industry on account of the demand of savvy and time-pressed consumers who were seeking a professional to take care of all of their financial needs.

Increased integration of financial intermediaries was facilitated by a rush of deregulation that began in the 1980s. The development of multi-functional financial intermediaries made it easier for companies to provide more comprehensive services to their customers. In the banking industry, consolidation was encouraged through the removal of a series of restrictions on intrastate and interstate banking, concluding with the Riefle-Neal Interstate Banking and Branching Efficiency Act of 1994.[6] The passage of the Gramm-Leach-Bliley Act removed the regulatory restrictions on bank involvement in underwriting, insurance and other "nonbank" activities which existed since the Banking Act of 1933 (relevant sections were known as the Glass-Steagall Act). Gramm-Leach-Bliley allowed the creation of a financial holding company under which subsidiaries can engage in insurance, securities and banking activities.

The market reacted well to the new legislation. In particular, shares of life insurance firms enjoyed a single-day average excess return of 4.9 percent.[7] This response demonstrated investor confidence that an increasingly

4.   Ibid, 8.

5.   Ibid, 5.

6.   Cara S. Loen, et al. (2000). "The Changing Policy of the Financial Services Industry: What Lies Ahead?" *Economic Policy Review Federal Reserve Bank of New York.* 6(4): 40.

7.   Ibid, 44.

integrated system of financial intermediaries would create value for both individual and institutional consumers. Years later, however, concerns mounted over financial services firms who have grown "too big to fail." In these so-called "supersize firms," problems in one division of the corporation threaten the integrity of the entire corporation and, in some cases, are believed to undermine the stability of the entire economic system. These concerns have led some politicians and regulators to consider repealing the Gramm-Leach-Bliley Act and establishing the barriers between banking and non-banking activities.

Gramm-Leach-Bliley Act
The Gramm-Leach-Bliley Act (GLBA) implemented the most sweeping overhaul of financial services regulation in the United States in over 60 years by eliminating the barriers between banking, investment banking, and insurance. It allows for affiliations between banks and other financial companies who may now establish so-called financial holding companies that can include commercial banking, securities underwriting, insurance underwriting, and merchant banking. This act lays the groundwork for significant further consolidation in the U.S. banking and financial industry.

Growth in Technology

Former Chairman of the Federal Reserve, Alan Greenspan, noted in a speech given in 2000 that, "without a doubt, the acceleration in technology that has produced such an extraordinary effect upon our economy in general has had a particularly profound impact in expanding the scope and utility of financial products over the last 15 years."[8]

Retail Banking Industry

The retail side of the financial services industry has perhaps been most affected by the growth of the Internet. Retail banking, in particular, has grown extraordinarily since the introduction of "PC Banking" in the 1990s. Banks developed proprietary systems that offered consumers the ability to perform simple transactions, such as checking balances and transferring funds. In

---

8. Alan Greenspan. (2000) "Technology and Financial Services." *Journal of Financial Services Research* 18(2/3): 109.

some cases, consumers were even able to pay bills and generate checks using additional software applications.[9]

The growth of the internet challenged previous business strategies. Banks were no longer able to depend on geographical proximity and "high switching" costs to ensure customer loyalty. Online banking in particular has reduced the role of physical geography in consumer's choice of banking services.[10] Consumers are able to identify the "loss-leaders" offered by financial firms and have become more savvy concerning various pricing strategies. Consumers are now able to deal with several different financial institutions, "cherry-picking" the products and services that best meet their needs.

Retail Brokerage Firms

Retail brokerage firms have transfored as a result of the Internet, principally through the emergence of low price online securities and free financial information services.[11] Technological advances created opportunities for growth in the online brokerage business through eliminating inefficiencies resulting from user-error and time-delays. Technology also enabled the separation of trading services from the advice giving services, which allowed brokerages to go after a new section of the market.[12] These financial gains have been partially offset by the imperative of aggressive advertising in order to attract and maintain consumers. However, advertising has been a double-edged sword since these campaigns also educate consumers of the prices they need to pay for transaction services. Consumers are better able to exert pressure on full-service brokers to earn their fees through adding significant value.

Insurance Companies

Technological advances in the insurance industry have not been as dramatic as those in the retail banking and brokerage sectors of the financial services industry. One significant change is increased price transparency resulting from the popularity of online price comparison services.

---

9. Eric K. Clemons and Lorin M. Hitt. (2000) "The Internet and the Future of Financial Services: Transparency, Differential Pricing and Disintermediation." *Center for Financial Institutions Working Papers* 00–35: 12.

10. Ibid, 14.

11. Ibid, 20.

12. Ibid, 21.

There are significant differences between the insurance industry and the retail banking and brokerage sectors, which hinder the prospects for growth on the Internet. The first difference is that insurance is primarily an "agent-driven" business, reaffirming the old adage that insurance is a "product which is sold and not bought." A second difference is due to the traditional compensation structure for insurance sales. Compensation is largely commission-based and experts speculate that agents may resist a direct distribution strategy via the internet. Insurance is a complex product and detailed personal information is needed to determine a quote on an insurance policy, particularly for life insurance. Therefore, insurance policies are less suited for internet-driven sales than other financial products, such as certificates of deposit. Finally, there are higher switching costs involved in changing insurance policies. This may cause consumers to seek out additional information on a face-to-face basis before making their selection.

Increased Reliance on Financial Services Professionals

Although recent decades witnessed an explosion of innovative financial products and the development of new markets, relatively few individuals have taken advantage of these opportunities to act as their own financial advisers. Some experts have noted that the increased depth and breadth of the financial system has coincided with a shift away from direct participation in financial markets and an increased reliance on intermediaries. In other words, individuals rely on financial services professionals and institutions to perform risk management on their behalf.[13]

While consumers have real-time access to more information than ever before, they increasingly depend upon professionals to interpret information and provide advice as to how to best achieve their financial goals. Technology has also opened up investment opportunities on a global scale to an extent never before possible; however, the sheer range of options can appear overwhelming to a non-expert. Consumers rely on professional advice to translate the raw data into information that can be used to make good decisions.

---

13. Allen and Santomero, 6.

Challenges for Financial Services Industry Professionals — Conflicts of Interest

A conflict of interest exists when a party to a transaction can gain by taking actions that are detrimental to its counterpart.[14] It is important to distinguish between conflicts of interest in which financial services professionals find themselves and conflicts of interest the professional creates through his or her actions. The former are distinguished from other conflicts of interests that are "built-in" to the structure of the system. Many of the "built-in" conflicts result from the multifunctional nature of the large financial firms. In these firms, there are pressures for various departments within the same firm to cooperate in ways which benefit the firm, but may not be in the best interest of the client.

Conflicts of interest are not necessarily unethical. For example, while it may be true that an agent may profit more from the sale of an unsuitable product than he would from selling a more suitable product, this does not entail that the agent would actually recommend the unsuitable product. In this case, a conflict exists, but this conflict is not exploited by the agent. Conflicts of interest present varying degrees of opportunity for financial services professionals to act in ways that are not in the interest of the client or the firm. That these opportunities exist is certainly not a desirable state of affairs and regulations, as well as professional codes of ethics, attempt to "neutralize" these temptations and align the interest of all parties. The financial services industry is unique because, unlike most other professions, a third party in most exchanges between a professional and his or her client is the firm by which the professional is employed.

As the following table indicates, some interest misalignments result from the structure of the financial services industry, namely, the presence of a financial firm as a third party in the professional/client relationship. Other conflicts originate in the specific policies utilized by various financial services firms. In both of these types, the ability of the financial services professionals to remove themselves entirely from the conflict is limited. However, professionals can certainly make a situation better or worse through their own actions and decisions. Through the course of this book, we will see examples of this.

---

14. Hamid Mehran and René M. Stulz. (2007) "The Economics of Conflicts of Interest in Financial Institutions." *Journal of Financial Economics* 85 (2): 267.

Possible Conflicts of Interest		
	Description	Example
Professional and the Client	Professional is incented to act in ways which do not benefit the client	Professional is compensated for selling client information to a 3rd party without the consent of the client
Institution, Professional and the Client	Institution creates policies which incent the professional to act in ways which benefit the institution at the expense of the client.	Company policy ties compensation to the sale of products which generate greater revenue for the company.
Institution and the Client	Institution develops products or institutes policies which benefits itself at the expense of the client. They do so in ways which may not explicitly benefit the professional and without the knowledge of the professional.	Company develops products/services which are misrepresented to the professional and through the professional to the client, i.e., develop misleading marketing materials or illustrations.
Professional and One or More Clients	Professional is incented to act in ways which benefit one client at the expense of other clients.	While advising multiple members of a single family, the professional acts in the interest of one client at the expense of the other client to whom it has the same obligations.
Institution and One or More Clients	Institution is incented to act in ways which benefit one client at the expense of other clients.	Company creates attractive investment opportunity for a high-value client at the expense of other clients to whom it has the same obligation

Manifestations of Conflicts of Interest

The misalignment of interest among the parties to an exchange or transaction in the financial services industry has been exploited by both practitioners and institutions. We will discuss the some of these manifestations in more detail as well as discuss steps professionals can take to extricate themselves from these conflicts or mitigate the potentially harmful effects of their exploitation.

One of the most frequent manifestations of misaligned interests emerges in the form of biased advice. As consumers increasingly depend on financial service professionals for advice, the opportunity for practitioners to exploit this dependence and make recommendations which benefit themselves at the expense of their clients increases as well. Since clients are often not in the position to assess the value and quality of the advice provided, there can be little to stop an unscrupulous practitioner from abusing the trust of his or her client. Professionals may have incentives to sell products which will result in higher profits for either themselves or the firm. Pressure can be applied by the firm to sell "house" products through offering incentives in the form of promotional and sales contests, cash awards or increased administrative support. Since the clients are typically unaware of incentive and compensation structures, they are unable to determine whether this product is truly in their best interest or whether another product would better serve their needs. Biases can operate below our immediate awareness of them which means a professional could be influenced by the incentive and compensation structure and yet not be fully aware of that influence. To the extent that various financial products are services that are priced differently, this conflict is built into the financial services industry and cannot easily be avoided.

EXAMPLE

Bias

An instance of a conflict of interest materializing as biased advice occurred among certain relationships between the brokerage research divisions and investment banking operations at some of the largest investment banks in the United States. As one commentator noted, "Analysts working for multi-functional financial firms wear several hats and are subject to multiple conflicts of interest.... These diverse roles are fundamentally incompatible, and raise intractable agency problems at the level of the individual analyst, the research function, the business unit and the financial firms as a whole."[15] Analysts are required to provide unbiased information and interpretation to investors; however, in many cases, analysts are also called upon to help raise capital for institutional clients in the securities origination and distribution process. These conflicting roles, essentially requiring analysts to serve two masters, investors and the firm, represent a conflict at the institutional level.

---

15. Ibid, 8.

In 2001, the issue of the compromised advice and recommendations provided by investment bank analysts came to a head.[16] After 2 years of investigation, the SEC announced in April 2003 that ten of the leading U.S. financial institutions agreed to pay $1.4 billion to settle violations of securities law ($875M in fines, $432.5 for research and $80M for consumer education).[17] The SEC enforcement action alleged that these firms "engaged in acts or practices that created or maintained inappropriate influence by investment banking over research analysts, thereby imposing conflicts of interest on research analysts." Among the charges was that analysts recommended investors buy stock in various companies while privately disparaging these same companies and their financial prospects.

According to the terms of the settlement, 10 investment banks are now required to limit contact between bankers and researchers and some analysts. Additionally, the investment banking industry agreed to a series of reforms, including the physical separation of research and investment banking, changes in the nature of analyst compensation contracts and strictures prohibiting analysts from attending road shows.

Involuntary Cross Selling

Involuntary cross-selling occurs in two ways. The first is when a client is pressured into acquiring additional products or services in order to access the product or service they actually want. An example may be the compelled purchase of credit insurance in order to secure a mortgage or a consumer loan. A conflict emerges when a client is uninformed as to the need or desirability of the additional product or service. There is a line between good salesmanship which may involve "up-selling" of a sort, and manipulating clients into purchasing products and services that they do not need. A second form of cross selling involves professionals applying the "default option" in ways which are not advantageous to the client, for example, placing client funds in a low interest rate or no interest rate, which may be profitable for your company, but not in the best interests of the client. Involuntary cross-selling, like biased advice, exploits the information asymmetry between professionals and their clients.

Excessive Trading, Churning and Twisting

Churning occurs when a professional initiates activity within a client's account or policy that does not benefit the client and only benefits the professional through generating fees. Excessive trading is essentially the same thing as churning, but refers to trades and activities being performed for the sake

---

16. Mark Tran, "$1.4 Billion Wall Street Settlement Finalized" Guardian.co.uk April 28, 2003. http://www.guardian.co.uk/business/2003apr.28.usnews. Accessed on June 23, 2009.
17. For additional information on the SEC complaint and settlement, http://www.sec.gov/news/speech/factsheet.htm.

of generating commissions. Churning occurs within accounts in which the professional has either formal discretionary control over the account or when the client is dependent upon the advice of the professional to such an extent that the professional can be said to have de facto discretionary control over the account. Actual discretionary control occurs when the client is unable to evaluate the professional's recommendations and exercise their own judgment.[18]

Churning can also occur in the sale of life insurance. In this case, an agent engages in churning when he or she persuades a client to drain a life insurance policy in order to fund a new policy with the same company with the purpose of generating commissions for the agent. Twisting occurs when the agent persuades the client to drain their current policy in order to purchase a new policy with another company, with the sole purpose of generating additional commissions for the agent.

Failure to Execute

When a financial services professional agrees to act as an agent for a client in a transaction, he or she is required to execute the wishes of the client in accordance with the client's instructions. For example, a broker is required to follow the instructions of their clients regarding any orders or trades within that client's account. Further, a broker is obliged to obtain the best price available for that client, within the limitations placed by his or her client.

A financial services professional who is selling life insurance can also be accused of a failure to execute. An example would be when a client purchases a life insurance policy and provides the premium payment to his or her agent. If the agent fails to record this payment and promptly turn over the payment to the issuing company, this agent fails to execute the orders of his or her client. This failure constitutes not only a lack of due diligence, but also represents a failure to maintain the commitment to act as the agent of the client. At its extreme, when the agent simply appropriates the client's payment for his or her own uses, this failure is an instance of fraud—but any misdirection or delay involving premium payments also constitutes a failure to execute.

---

18. Churning and Excessive Trading are governed under SEC Rule 15c-7 and FINRA Rule 2310 and FINRA Rule 2310-2 (b)(2).

Insufficient or Misleading Disclosure

Insufficient disclosure occurs when the financial services professional fails to disclose all of the information which is necessary for a reasonable person to make a decision whether a financial product, service or strategy is in his or her best interest. Disclosure is misleading when information is conveyed to the client in a manner that either confuses or obfuscates the true meaning or relevance of the information disclosed. Both insufficient and misleading disclosures make it more difficult for the client to act in his or her own best interest. This refusal to be truthful and candid is particularly harmful in the financial services industry because many clients are not sophisticated enough to ask the questions to obtain the information they need to know to make a good decision. Information is typically withheld from the client in an effort to persuade the client to act in such a way that they would not act if they had all of the relevant information. In effect, the financial services practitioner is picking and choosing what information to disclose so that the client acts in the way the agent desires, usually to benefit themselves or their company.

EXAMPLE

An example of misleading disclosures or sales tactics within the life insurance industry concerns the misuse of illustrations in the 1980s and 1990s. Illustrations are provided by agents or the issuing carrier to help clients understand how their life insurance policy works. While illustrations appear to have a veneer of certainty, they are best described as hypothetical representations which use assumptions the company uses to compute the policy results.[19] Industry practitioners have argued that illustrations are an invaluable tool in explaining to clients the features of their policy; however, ethical problems emerged when practitioners failed to explain the hypothetical nature of these illustrations and their assumptions. Instead, some practitioners presented illustrations as guarantees of performance.

---

19. Neil Alexander, "Understanding Life Insurance Illustrations: How to Make Sense of It All?" *Journal of Accountancy* 195(2): 70.

In the 1990s, many consumers were surprised to discover that policies they believed would be fully paid off in just a few years, still required heavy premium payments to remain in force. A downward spiral of interest rates undermined insurance company estimates for how long it would take for the premium payment to vanish, that is, to be fully covered by the dividends and interest payments paid on the cash value of the policy.[20] So-called "vanished premiums" emerged with devastating consequences for individuals who were not prepared to fund the required premium payments. In 1995, the National Association of Insurance Commissioners (NAIC) adopted the Life Insurance Illustrations Model Regulation, which was designed to eliminate some of the ethical issues concerning the inappropriate use of illustrations.[21] Ethical infractions ranged from well intended agents who perhaps neglected to perform sufficient due diligence on the illustrations provided to them by the carrier to unscrupulous individuals who manipulated illustrations in order to initiate unnecessary new sales. The case of deceptive illustrations points to the difficulty that well intended financial services professionals often face when dealing with company and industry practices which make it difficult to act in the best interests of their clients. The widespread and often negative publicity which emerged as a result of the inappropriate use of illustrations damaged the credibility of the insurance industry and undermined public faith in the integrity of insurance professionals and corporations.

Violation of Privacy/Breaches of Confidentiality

Clients are encouraged to be open and candid with their financial services professional, both about the current state of their financial affairs and their financial goals and objectives. In order for a professional to help clients maintain their financial health and achieve long term goals, it is necessary for a client to disclose personal information about themselves and their family members. The expectation is that this information will be used by the professional only to enable him or her to work more effectively in the best interests of the client. When professionals use the personal information shared by their clients for their own gain, they violate the promise of confidentiality upon which the success of the financial services industry depends.

Given the value of personal information and data for marketing purposes, individual financial services professionals may be tempted to sell or trade confidential client information to third parties. An example may be a financial services professional who sells the personal information of his or her "high-value" clients to an accountant or attorney who is interested in doing a targeted marketing campaign. Privacy issues have become increasingly

20.   Amey Stone. (1993) "Police Your Policy Now" *Business Week:* 108.
21.   Edward P. Mohoric. (1998) "Overview of the Life Insurance Model Regulation. "*Journal of the American Society of CLU and ChFC.* 52(3): 52.

important as financial intermediaries evolve to multifunctional institutions and are therefore able to have several levels of interaction with an individual client.

Unsuitable Products

Clients depend upon the advice and recommendations of financial services professionals, and they are vulnerable to unscrupulous practitioners who trade off the trust and ignorance of their clients and sell and recommend products which are not appropriate for their needs. While it is impossible to collect and process information about every financial product on the market, it is reasonable to expect that financial services professionals, who present themselves as experts, have an understanding of financial products and markets that is both wide and deep. Simply adopting a "one size fits all" approach to recommending and selling products is not ethically appropriate and fails to meet a professional's commitment to his or her clients.

At times, financial service firms fail to develop suitable products. A failure to develop suitable products occurs when the product lines offered by a specific company are not adequate to meet the needs of the market that they purport to serve, either because the products are poorly designed and not competitive with other products in the marketplace, or because the products are designed to meet a far narrower segment of the marketplace than the subset to whom the company markets its products. If financial services professionals are not confident that the products offered by their company are adequate to meet the needs of their clients, they have an ethical responsibility to develop a solution to this conflict. This conflict is particularly troublesome if the professional is employed as a captive agent.

Objectives of This Course

This course has three objectives:

1. Explain the specific obligations of financial services professionals.
2. Explain the ethical problems and challenges faced by professionals within the financial services industry.
3. Present the argument that ethical behavior is required for the long-term profitability and sustainability of the financial services professional, financial services firms and the financial services industry in general.

Members of the financial services industry play a crucial role in assisting their clients plan for and maintain their financial security. Clients rely on the advice provided by their financial services professionals to make sound decisions about their financial needs, goals and future. Society depends on the work of financial service professionals to ensure that its citizens are able to maintain healthy and independent lives even in times of economic hardship, uncertainty and loss. This dependence on the profession as a whole, and individual financial services professionals specifically, is based on the belief that their trust is well-placed and that they can have confidence in the integrity of the professionals with whom they work and organizations charged with regulating their behavior. There is a presumption that financial services professionals will conduct business fairly and in accordance with the highest ethical principles. When professionals violate this trust, society demands that these individuals are reprimanded and sanctioned by the members of their profession and the appropriate regulatory authorities.

At times, individual financial services professionals and the industry as a whole have failed this trust. Certain individual professionals have not conducted business in accordance with the highest ethical principles and many people have been seriously harmed by their misdeeds. Professional organizations and regulatory bodies compounded this breach of trust by failing to appropriately police and sanction those individuals. Throughout its history, the financial services profession has been forced to regain the trust of the society it is mandated to serve. The unfortunate result is that the ethical breaches of a few unscrupulous individuals caused reverberations throughout the entire industry.

The best and most sure way to earn and maintain the trust of individual clients and society at large is through a demonstrated commitment to conducting business in accordance with the highest ethical principles. Empirical evidence demonstrates that individuals and corporations who structure their business practices in accordance with ethical principles succeed and prosper financially. In this sense, ethical principles are truly sustainable principles, and the ethical professional is also the prudent and wise practitioner. These statements are particularly true regarding the financial services industry, the success of which depends on earning and maintaining the trust of the people it serves. Financial services professionals do not sell tangible and material products, the value of which consumers can confidently assess. Financial services professionals sell advice and the promise of future security and well being, intangible goods whose value is more ambiguous. Within the financial services industry, trust and confidence often is placed in the character of the financial services professional and the reputation of the company with which he or she is affiliated, rather than in the value of a complex and often incomprehensible financial product.

While financial success inevitably follows upon ethical business practices in the long term, many people who dedicate their careers to acting as financial services professionals are motivated by goods beyond profit. It is certainly possible to "do well by doing good," but most financial services professionals desire to act ethically for simple reason that it is the right thing to do. Most financial services professionals recognize both the vulnerability of their clients and their dependence on the products, services and advice they provide. Many strive to be worthy of the trust that is placed in them. These professionals seek to move beyond acting in accordance with the letter of the law and strive to fulfill the spirit of the law in their actions. It is our goal that this text, and this course, will serve as the foundation you need to develop the skills that will enable you to meet the ethical challenges you will face with integrity and in accordance with the highest ethical principles.

Chapter Review Questions

Answers to Review Questions are in the Appendix.

1. According to Solomon Huebner, the founder of The American College, which of the characteristics below is <u>not</u> a trait that distinguishes salespersons and other practitioners from professionals?

    (A) abandoning your beliefs for those of your company
    (B) a useful vocation
    (C) having a spirit of loyalty to other professionals
    (D) a vocation that involves a science

2. What does failure to execute mean?

    (A) broker misses a scheduled client meeting
    (B) broker deliberately manipulates the orders and instructions of their clients in order to produce some financial gain or material advantage for themselves or their firm.
    (C) broker signs documents for his client
    (D) broker gives legal advice to client

3.   This ethics course has been developed to help financial services
     professionals

     (A)   respond to the increased legal pressure that the public has placed
           upon them
     (B)   respond to the expectations and responsibilities the public has placed
           upon them
     (C)   deal with the allegations with which the public has charged them
     (D)   help insurance companies, banks and securities firms deflect their
           increased exposure to legal liability

4.   The Gramm-Leach-Bliley Act caused

     (A)   the deregulation of the insurance industry
     (B)   the construction of barriers between the banking, investment banking
           and insurance industries
     (C)   the elimination of barriers between the banking, investment banking
           and insurance industries
     (D)   the reversal of the McCarran-Ferguson Act

5.   What best describes a conflict of interest in the financial service industry?

     (A)   agents using illustrations that may be deceptive in nature
     (B)   agent personally gains by selling something to a client that will hurt
           the client
     (C)   agents omission of facts to the client's detriment
     (D)   agents selling products without a clear understanding of them

6.   When an agent sells or recommends products which not appropriate for
     client needs, this is an example of

     (A)   unsuitability on the part of the client
     (B)   fraud
     (C)   decreased legal liability and career risks
     (D)   lying on the part of the agent

7.   Which of the following is not an effect on the financial services industry due to
     the growth of the internet?

     (A)   increase in fraudulent checks
     (B)   better communication
     (C)   better customer access
     (D)   better marketing to consumers

READ THE FOLLOWING DIRECTIONS BEFORE CONTINUING

The questions below differ from the preceding questions in that they all contain the word EXCEPT. So you understand fully the basis used in selecting each answer, be sure to read each question carefully.

---

8. All of the following are major unethical practices in which the abuse of professionalism has occurred EXCEPT

    (A) misuse of illustrations
    (B) necessary policy replacement
    (C) product misrepresentation
    (D) forgery

9. All of the following are major ethical requirements facing the financial services professional EXCEPT

    (A) proper identification of skills
    (B) identifying and meeting customer needs
    (C) the need for compliance training
    (D) honest marketing

10. All of the following are key factors that have contributed to the changes in the financial services marketplace over the past 10 years EXCEPT

    (A) technological advancements
    (B) a changing legal environment
    (C) an increase in the financial services workforce
    (D) the integration of financial services

Learning Objectives

An understanding of the material in this chapter should enable the student to

1. Analyze his or her level of ethical sensitivity.

ETHICS AND ETHICAL SENSITIVITY

What is ethics? Ethics deals with the question, "What should one do?" It doesn't apply in all situations, of course, for you can ask, "Should one put the fork on the left or the right of the plate?" or "How often should one change the oil in a car?" or "Should one add more color to the corner of the painting to give it balance?" Those are simply cases of etiquette, car maintenance, and aesthetics. Ethics deals with what people should do in situations where actions can seriously affect their own well-being or the well-being of others. If you put the fork on the right, no person's well-being is seriously affected for better or worse. If you fire a loyal employee, however, that employee's well-being is seriously affected.

The word *ethics* is derived from the ancient Greek word *ethos,* which means "customs or habits." Ethics, therefore, refers to the rules by which people live or the customary way of doing something. The word *morals,* which for all practical purposes is synonymous with ethics, is derived from the Latin word *mores* and also refers to societal customs and rules.

Any society requires rules to exist in an orderly fashion and will have its own ethics or mores. To the extent that it successfully socializes or civilizes its members, that set of rules will be incorporated into the thinking processes and attitudes of the group's members. Hence, any adult of any group comes equipped with a set of moral or ethical rules that he or she has "inherited" from his or her culture. For them, certain actions will be "acceptable" or "good" or "right," and certain actions will be "unacceptable" or "bad" or "wrong." The purpose of those societal rules is, of course, to make the society an orderly place so that people can get along and thrive.

People internalized the rules and customs of their societies while they were growing up, sometimes to such an extent that they were not even aware that they were following those rules and customs. They learned appropriate behavior long ago, and internalized it so much that their behavior is automatic. Consider how many people, without even thinking about it, bring a notebook to class and automatically take notes. While the practice of taking notes is not an ethical practice that gives rise to an ethical rule, as an example it is indicative of how people follow rules they have internalized without thought. Most of us learned our ethical rules or principles at home, in our schools, through the religious institutions with which we are affiliated, through the stories we were told or read, or through what we absorbed from the media, such as television.

Thus, the term ethics often refers to those rules or mores people use to guide their lives. Those rules are embedded in a society's ways of life and are learned and modified by individuals who have different beliefs derived from different sources and modified by individual reactions to life experience. But the term ethics can also refer to a branch of philosophy, a study concerned with principles or rules of conduct and their foundations. One of the purposes of this book is to present some of those principles and attempt to apply them to specific life situations.

For those in financial services, there are two major areas of practical application: everyday life and business life. Wherever we look, we find three kinds of situations. One type of situation is a "no brainers" in which it is very clear what is right and what is wrong. Another type of situation is a dilemma that is complicated and in which principles or rules conflict. Finally, there are situations where we might not even be aware that we are facing an ethical issue.

To begin we will review some concrete situations. We will see examples where there are conflicting promises or commitments, conflicts between doing what a client wants and what a client needs, and actions that are simultaneously harmful and beneficial to people.

AN ETHICAL SENSITIVITY EXERCISE

As previously noted, ethics can pose fundamental questions such as: What should I do? What sort of person should I be? What sort of life or activities will fulfill me and make me happy? What sorts of actions are right or wrong? We often need to decide whether acting in a certain way is or is not ethical.

That is when we exercise our ethical judgment, and we will have a great deal to say about what sound ethical judgment is in the next chapter.

In the exercise that follows, you will consider actions to determine how sensitive you are to some ethical issues. To indicate how you feel, put a check in the appropriate box to indicate the degree of your reservations about performing the action described in the exercise.

- If you have no ethical reservations about the action described, put a check in the box labeled "None."
- If you have serious reservations about performing the action, put a check in the box labeled "Major."
- If you have only have minor reservations about the action, check the box labeled "Minor."
- If you have more moderate reservations about performing the action, check the box labeled "Moderate."

Some of these scenarios might be a bit ambiguous. That is okay for now. We will worry about the ambiguity later. Just use your imagination to fill in the blanks in each scenario so you will be able to indicate your level of ethical concern.

Now, look at each of the scenarios in the Ethical Sensitivity Awareness Exercise which follows and check the box that best represents your level of ethical concern. We'll explain the scoring after the exercise.

	Test Your Ethical Sensitivity/Awareness					
		\multicolumn{4}{}{Level of Ethical Concern}			
	Ethical Dilemma	**None**	**Minor**	**Moderate**	**Major**	**Score**
1.	You don't inform a wife, who is your client and has limited ability to manage funds, when her husband asks your help in getting a codicil in his will drafted which will increase the amount put in trust for the minor children.					
2.	You take full credit for an ingenious use of a product that one of your agents developed.					
3.	You inform the children of an elderly man about the erratic changes he has made in his will. A recent widower, he asked you to change his will to leave most of his money to the SPCA, with whose director he claims to have fallen deeply in love. The director's son, a financial planner, will make the changes if you do not.					
4.	You give NFL box seat tickets to the human resource director of a company to expedite negotiations on an employee benefits package you want to sell to that company. (Such gifts are an expected perk in the director's company.)					
5.	You join a service club in the city where your agency operates in order to network.					
6.	You advise your client's husband how to reduce her share of his estate because he thinks she is suffering from dementia. Its his second marriage and there are no children, and your client has her own assets.					
7.	You give your wife a gift to make up for not going with her to the theater as you promised, because you had to meet with a client who had asked for an impromptu meeting.					
8.	You don't mention a replacement product's downside to a client.					
9.	You lower fees for services for new clients without a corresponding rate decrease for older clients.					
10.	You put off completing the annual financial report for your child's scouting organization so that you can finish a presentation to an important client.					
11.	You indicate on a life insurance application that a client is a nonsmoker, even though you know he smokes.					

Ethical Dilemma	Level of Ethical Concern				Score
	None	Minor	Moderate	Major	
12. You provide a friend with confidential knowledge that your company plans to merge so he can buy stock in the company, thus making a quick profit on the merger.					
13. You bring a competent colleague in to help you with a planning case that is a bit beyond your reach because you feel the client doesn't trust you to do it alone.					
14. You decide to use a financial planner of dubious competency from your multidisciplinary firm to help you with a difficult case, even though you know that there is a more capable planner available who is not part of your firm.					
15. You encourage your client to sign multiple fund transfer forms in blank and give you verbal approval to use them at your discretion.					
16. You turn over your lower-income clients, to whom you promised originally to serve as their lifelong agent, to a junior colleague because you don't have time to manage their accounts adequately, which are not large enough to be worth your while financially.					
17. You do not reveal information to your manager about the possible market conduct violations of one of the producers affiliated with your office.					
18. You place a young agent under the supervision of a mentor to improve his production prior to his possible dismissal.					
19. You set up a charitable remainder trust for the benefit of your client and offer it to a charity for a commission of 5 percent of the funding amount.					
20. You expedite the transactions for a middle-aged client with minimal investment experience who insists on investing a significant portion of her total assets in high-risk funds.					
Your Score	x0	+x1	+x2	+x3	= Total

Test Your Ethical Sensitivity/Awareness, continued

YOUR RESPONSES TO THESE SCENARIOS

Areas of Agreement

Because ethics is basically a social enterprise where we learn the rules from the society or groups in which we live, we should expect that we will agree with each other on a great deal of the issues. In our work with people on these scenarios we do find such agreement. It is important to note that without a great deal of agreement—what we call unanimity (likeness of spirit)—ethics would not be impossible. We will address this issue in a later chapter.

In the following discussion, we will indicate those areas where we have found a great deal of agreement and try to indicate why this is so. That will give us some foundations in ethics to build on.

No Reservations

Let's look first at areas where most people would probably agree. To begin, we bet there were some scenarios in which you had no reservations. Did you have any difficulties with number 5, joining the local service club? Probably not. Most people don't. Service organizations help people. Why would you have a problem with someone joining one? Doing good is laudatory. But wait. Every once in a while someone has a problem with your joining a service club, because doing so helps your business networking. They are objecting to your doing a good thing for the wrong reasons. They are considering an aspect of an ethical issue that is very subtle. You not only should do the right thing, but you should also do it for the right reasons.

Did you have any difficulty with number 13, bringing in a competent colleague to help you with a planning case that is a bit beyond your reach because you feel the client doesn't trust you to do it alone? Isn't that exactly what the competency requirement of most codes of ethics would demand? If you aren't competent, you should get help.

Let's look at another scenario. How about number 18? You are placing a young agent under a mentor's supervision to improve his production prior to possible dismissal. What could be wrong with that? It seems like you are trying to help someone with potential who desperately needs assistance to fulfill that potential. Some might think that such an action is going too far for a manager, being too nice, but by and large, most people would have no reservations about such activity.

These are three scenarios about which most people would agree they have no reservations. And that should tell us some things about ethics. The first thing is that there are areas in ethics where all, or most, people agree. The second thing is that all of ethics is not about the hard cases. Ethics permeates all of our lives. It deals with the good actions and the bad actions of people. There are things we do that we are supposed to do, and we should have no reservations about doing them. At best, we should have reservations about *not* doing them.

Serious Reservations

How about number 2, taking full credit for a product that one of your agents developed? Most people think that is wrong. It is not fair and it does harm to your peer by taking credit away from him and giving it to you. You may not have marked it as causing serious reservations, but our guess is that you at least had moderate reservations about such an action.

How about number 11, filling out a life insurance application for a client whom you know to be a smoker? You indicate she is a nonsmoker because she claims your job is simply to write down the answers she gives. She'll find another agent if you don't do it. Most people have serious reservations about this. Why? Because it involves lying, and most of us think, rightly so, that it's wrong to lie, even if you do it to help a client and yourself.

How about number 12, mentioning to a friend confidential knowledge that your company plans to merge so your friend can buy stock in the company? Most people with whom we discuss this will have serious reservations about such activity because it involves insider trading, a practice that is illegal.

How about number 15, encouraging a client to sign blank multiple fund transfer forms and to give you verbal approval to use them at your discretion? Most people from the insurance industry have serious reservations about this behavior. The reason so many agents have reservations about it is because of the abuse of this business practice, including window paning that took place back in the late 1970s, 1980s, and early 1990s.

There may be other scenarios with which you have serious reservations, and we will get to those. For now, though, we are concentrating on the situations upon which all people agree, whether it is agreement about having serious reservations or having no reservations. If you have serious reservations about scenarios 2, 11, 12, and 15, you are in agreement with a large number of fellow financial services professionals. And if you have no reservations about 5, 13, and 18, you are also in agreement with a large number of your fellow financial services professionals. What this agreement shows is that there is unanimity, a like-mindedness, about ethical issues. And we contend that where there is like-mindedness about ethical issues, there is an ethical community or culture. After all, the word ethics comes from ethos, which means culture; the word morals comes from mores, which means the way of doing things. Groups each have a culture which imbues in them ways of doing things. These ways of doing things are the general guidelines by which the people in a culture live.

Given that, one of the things we will do in this course is to look at issues concerning which there is a great deal of agreement about proper ethical behavior—what we call "no brainers." We use the somewhat nontechnical term "no-brainer" to indicate a situation in which it is clear what should or should not be done and why. For example, you should not falsify an application because that is a lie.

However, it's important to note that, just because we shouldn't do something doesn't mean we won't go ahead and do it. We are all familiar with the phenomenon of doing something we know is wrong. None of us is perfect, but the fact that we do something wrong, or that a lot of people do something wrong, doesn't make it right. We will return to this issue.

Areas of Disagreement

In addition to those areas in which we have agreement, there are those with which there is legitimate and real disagreement. I've assumed agreement about scenarios 2, 5, 11, 12, 13, 15, and 18. That comprises more than a third of the scenarios. But it also leaves about two-thirds for which there is usually some disagreement.

1. Sometimes there is disagreement because we just don't have enough facts.
2. Sometimes there is disagreement because we operate by different sets of rules.
3. And sometimes there is disagreement because there is some deep conflict about values and/or principles.

Let's briefly look at each of the remaining scenarios and at the possible reasons for the disagreement.

Scenario 1—not informing a wife about her husband's request that you help him get a codicil to his will drafted which will increase the amount put in trust for the minor children. The wife appears to have limited ability to manage funds. This scenario usually generates a great deal of discussion and disagreement because it involves a complexity of relationships. Are both the wife and the husband clients? If so, do you need to inform the wife about the husband's request? Can you continue to be an advisor to both of them? How far does confidentiality bind you when it requires you to keep the confidence of one client which may violate the other client's right to know what is happening to her portfolio?

Scenario 3—informing the children of an elderly male client about his strange, erratic behavior. (A recent widower, he asked you to arrange to have his will changed to leave most of his money to the SPCA, with whose director he claims to have fallen deeply in love.) This raises questions similar to those in scenario one about confidentiality. What is your responsibility to your client, who is likely suffering from some sort of dementia? Do you follow his wishes if you suspect he is not capable of making decisions for his own benefit? How seriously are you bound by the rule to look out for a client's best interests, particularly when those best interests will not be served if you accede to the client's wishes? Who are you to determine what is in the client's best interest? Shouldn't you just do what the client asks even if, in your best professional judgment, it is not suitable? In discussing this case with producers, we have found people on all sides of the issue. It is an extremely complicated case which demands we take into account all sorts of issues.

Scenario 4—giving box seat NFL tickets to the human resource director of a company to expedite the adoption of an employee benefits package you are pushing. (This would be an expected perk in his company.) There is usually disagreement when evaluating this action, and it can generate much discussion. Is giving tickets to a client to encourage him to give you business appropriate? Is it similar to a bribe or extortion? Or is it just the way we do business? Is it okay if you are an RIA (Registered Investment Advisor)? After all, there is a monetary limit to the size of gift you can accept. Would this be okay if it were tickets to a minor league baseball game instead of an NFL game? Tickets to minor league baseball games are much less expensive than those to NFL games. What are the rules governing the giving and receiving of gifts for insurance agents, financial planners, and investment advisors? Are they the same or not? Here we need more facts. We also need specific knowledge of the particular rules of the associations to which you belong.

Scenario 6—advising your client's husband how to minimize his wife's share of his estate because he thinks his wife, your client, suffers from dementia.

It's his second marriage, there are no children, and your client has her own assets. The scenario involves violating your client's rights to your services, but it is probably for the long-run benefit of both her and her husband. Here, more facts are needed about your relationship to the husband and the client in order to decide what to do. This case raises questions about how to serve both clients' best interests and how much you are bound by the confidentiality and fiduciary issues involved.

Scenario 7—substituting a gift for a theater date with your spouse because you have to meet with a client for an impromptu meeting. This scenario raises an issue about what to do when faced with a conflict of loyalties, if not conflicting commitments. If you promised your spouse a theater date, aren't you breaking that promise? Isn't your word your bond? There is an ever-growing concern over the struggle between the demands of a personal life and the demands of a business life. How are we to resolve these competing demands? We utilize this seemingly harmless scenario, to point out that there are times in your life when you have urgent but conflicting obligations? What are you to do then? It would seem wise to do that which promotes the most good or avoids the most harm. But is that sufficient to justify breaking commitments? We will look at these issues more carefully in the next chapter.

Scenario 8—not mentioning or adequately discussing the replacement of your client's old traditional life policy prior to her signing an application for a new policy, because of her busy schedule. There is a general consensus that this is, at least, moderately problematic. Most professionals suggest it is the agent's responsibility to insist that the client make the time to meet with the agent. If the client refuses, the agent should not finalize the transaction. But there are those who maintain that it is the client's decision about how informed the client should be.

Scenario 9—lowering fees for services for new clients without a corresponding rate decrease for older clients. This generates a great deal of disagreement because lower fees mean less income. The question revolves around what is fair. While some think this is unfair to the older clients, others think it is a perfectly acceptable way to obtain new business. What often comes up in the discussions of this scenario is self-examination about whether one is in the transactional business (i.e., simply involved in selling a product to a customer), or in the relationship building business (i.e., attempting to establish long term relationships with clients).

Scenario 10—delaying completion of an annual financial report needed by your child's scouting organization so you can complete an important client presentation. Here you are faced with a common ethical problem: a conflict of obligations, which arises because you promised to do two things and find yourself in the situation in which the two promises conflict. You cannot keep one without breaking the other. You have an obligation both to the scout club and to the client. Who gets precedence? The disagreements about what to do are often solved with more information. If the annual report is not due immediately, you can postpone it because no one will be harmed. If it can't be postponed, you may have to delay the client presentation. Life is complicated and conflicts of obligation arise quite often. They are not always easy to resolve. One of the goals of this course is to give you some tools that will enable you to evaluate a situation and perhaps come up with a practical solution that is also an ethical one.

Scenario 14—deciding to use a financial planner, whose judgment you question, from your multidisciplinary firm to help you with a difficult case, even though you know there is a more capable planner available who is not part of your firm. This raises a serious question faced by those who work, or are contemplating working, in multidisciplinary financial planning firms. Is one's obligation more to the firm than to the client? What do you do when your employer insists that you use the company's personnel? There are similarities here with the cases where one is a captive agent of a company, and where one's primary obligation is to the company. In that case how does one look out for the interest of the client? This is a classic conflict of interest case. How are we to handle those?

Scenario 16—turning over your lower-income clients to a junior colleague because you don't have time to service their accounts adequately, and they are not lucrative enough to be worth your while financially. You originally promised those clients you would be their lifelong agent. This is a situation with which more and more high-end agents wrestle. They made such a promise, but their C and D clients now get in the way of adequately servicing their A and B clients. If they terminate their C and D clients it looks like they are breaking their original commitment to be their lifelong agent. It appears to involve breaking one's word to the client. Of course, some argue that it is in the client's best interest to step aside and let the clients be serviced by someone who can give them more time. At any rate, it raises the issue of what would be a good reason for setting aside or not abiding by a promise. Are there times when it is alright not to do what one promised to do?

Scenario 17—not revealing information to your manager about possible market conduct violations of one of the producers affiliated with your office. This circumstance raises issues about whether and when we are ethically obliged to blow the whistle to keep our profession ethical and honorable. Obviously, because deciding when and if blowing the whistle is required is such a hard issue, one can expect much disagreement about this course of action. But the fact that you are probably troubled about what you should do, indicates that you think there is some obligation to police the profession in which you work.

Scenario 19—setting up a charitable remainder trust for your client and offering it to a charity for a commission of 5 percent of the funding amount. Such compensation creates conflicts of interest. When this issue is addressed by those whose main work is charitable giving, there is usually agreement that this is a serious breach of ethics, and they have serious reservations.

Scenario 20—going along with a middle-aged client with minimal investment experience who insists on investing a significant portion of her total assets in high-risk funds. This action raises the issue of what it means to look out for the client's best interest, particularly when what the client wants is clearly not in her own best interest. If a product is not suitable, can I sell it to a client anyway, simply because the client wants it? Or does my professional status require that I refuse to do what is clearly not in my client's best interest? Some producers even ask if it is necessary to terminate the relationship with the client if he or she does not take your advice on this issue. All agree that, if you do go along with the client, you need to get his or her permission in writing, out of your own self interest.

These are the kind of issues one is likely to encounter in the day to day activity of a financial planner. Some are troublesome and some are easy. They are presented to you for your consideration and treatment. Discussing these scenarios, deciding what you believe, and discovering what specific rules govern your behavior are the central activities of ethical analysis.

How to Score the Exercise

This activity should help you to discover how sensitive you are to the ethical dimension of some situations you face in your day-to-day existence. Some people are too sensitive; some are probably not sensitive enough. If you want to compare yourself to others, add up your score—you get zero points for None, one point for Minor, two points for Moderate, and three points for Major. The majority of planners who have done this exercise fall in the range of twenty-nine to thirty-six. We make no claims for its scientific validity; simply use this range as a guide for how you compare with a large number of other financial services professionals.

Look at the figure below. Wherever you fall in the sensitivity range, it is important to be aware of two things. First, be aware that every action has an ethical dimension; and second, that there are certain factors—like fairness, commitment, and benefiting or harming people—that make a situation an ethical one. We will turn to those considerations now, by briefly discussing the nature of ethics. This will give us some ethical decision-making tools that we can apply in examining issues we will discuss in the rest of the book.

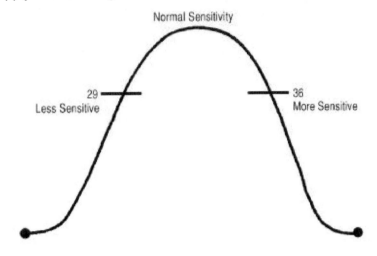

Learning Objectives

An understanding of the material in this chapter should enable the student to

1. Achieve a better understanding of what "ethics" means.

2. Identify the possible consequences of and penalties for unethical conduct by the financial services professional.

3. Identify the six questions used in making ethical decisions, which rest upon the four major principles.

4. Describe what the role of morality is and why commitment is so important.

ETHICS

There is historical evidence that moral codes have existed at all times and in all places. They are a necessary part of the human order, and without them there would be chaos. These codes have been applied in various forms in diverse situations and circumstances, and have developed in different ways. Some moral codes developed in conjunction with religious beliefs. Others developed as a result of customs to promote human harmony. For example, in ancient Egypt, strong secular leaders established precepts which, in combination with a strict religion, affected the behavior of all members of Egyptian society. In Israel, the Judaic religion guided moral behavior. Its tenets were spelled out in the commandments of the Mosaic law and members of Hebrew society were expected to follow these standards without question. Early Christian thought focused on the role of God to achieve good—God's help was necessary; will and intelligence alone were insufficient. In whatever way moral codes developed, it is instructional to remember how similar the various moral codes are. All the major religions of the world share a common theme expressed in the Golden Rule, "Do unto others as you would have them do unto you."

The Golden Rule
The Golden Rule is a universal ethical norm, utilized by most, if not all, the major religions. Consider the following six versions.

1. Good people proceed while considering that what is best for others is best for themselves (Hitopadesa, Hinduism).

2. Thou shalt regard thy neighbor as thyself (Leviticus 19:18, Judaism).

3. All things whatsoever ye would that men should do to you, do ye even so to them (Matthew 7:12, Christianity).

4. Hurt not others with that which pains yourself. (Udanavarga 5:18, Buddhism)

5. What you do not want done to yourself, do not do to others (Analects 15:23, Confucianism).

6. No one of you is a believer until he loves for his brother what he loves for himself (Traditions, Islam).

Some of the greatest systematizers of ethics were the Ancient Greek thinkers like Socrates, Plato, Aristotle and the Stoics. They were the first philosophers to speculate theoretically about what constitutes right and wrong behavior and helped identify some of the major principles underlying most moral codes.

Modern thinkers, like John Locke, held that ethics was embedded in a natural law and provided a sort of social contract that gives us guidance on how to flourish in society. Adam Smith, in *The Wealth of Nations,* sketched out an ethical framework for modern business. It is often called the enlightened self-interest model. Smith claimed that the free enterprise system, which espouses liberty and autonomy, works and has prospered because it benefits the common good, when constrained by justice. However, in whatever historical era, ethics has always consisted of a set of beliefs about what is right and wrong. We will examine these different beliefs and see how they are related. Before that, though, let's address the question of why ethics is important.

WHY ETHICS IS IMPORTANT IN THE FINANCIAL SERVICES

There are those who feel that ethics is an esoteric subject, one reserved for scholars and not for business people. Some say, "There's no such thing as business ethics." They say that business ethics is an oxymoron, a contradiction in terms. But what are those people indicating? Do they think it's okay to cheat? Do they think stealing is acceptable? Do they think that misrepresentation is acceptable? Do they think that trust in business is not necessary? Not really. When pressed, they admit that ethics is absolutely essential to running a business well. Without ethics in business, there would be no trust. Without ethics, no one would keep promises. There would be no reliability. It would be a dog-eat-dog world of the survival of the fittest. There would be no real giving of advice, which requires looking out for the interest of the advisee, before the interest of the advisor. What they mean to say is that they have seen instances where people in business cheat or steal or misrepresent. But they will also insist that they don't do such things. If they did it would be silly in the extreme because no one would trust them and do business with them. As we have said, ethics is necessary for, and allows, human beings to get along together so they can flourish. This is particularly applicable in the financial services industry.

When a member of the public buys a financial product, the very nature of the transaction is usually lopsided. It involves what is called "knowledge asymmetry." The agent generally knows far more about the product than the client. The contract is drafted by the company, not by competing teams of attorneys representing both sides. Trust is the key ingredient. Without a sense of trust that (1) the agent is looking out for the client's interest, (2) the agent is fairly representing the product and (3) the company will honor its obligations, few consumers would be willing to purchase financial products like insurance, annuities, mutual funds or stocks. Trust is an elusive concept. It takes years to build, but it can be torn down quickly. When the scandals of the Madoffs of the world or the AIGs or the Enrons come to light, people lose trust in the integrity of the financial markets.

The financial services industry is now at a crossroads. Over the years, the industry has honored its obligations and consumers have had faith in what they were told in sales presentations. Unfortunately, recent events have now undermined this trust. The need to restore public trust is urgent. Our livelihoods is at stake. Each person working in the financial services area has a role in this process. Our actions and the way we conduct our business affairs must become important parts of the equation. Restoring the public trust involves going beyond the mere letter of the law to a full-fledged effort on the part of agents to act in an ethical manner—to take that extra step to do what is right. Good ethics is good business.

PENALTIES FOR UNETHICAL BEHAVIOR

Not only is good ethics good business for building trust, there is a self-interested reason for behaving ethically. There can be legal penalties and liability issues that arise when one acts unethically.

As we have learned from the Bernie Madoffs of the world and the Enron and WorldCom scandals, the penalties for ethical lapses are severe. Not every breach of ethics is detected, but where unethical behavior is discovered, its costs can more than outweigh any potential gains. Ethical breaches end careers more quickly and more definitively than any other lapse in business judgment. The proof is in the headlines of articles on the financial services scandals. How many of those professionals will ever work in financial services again?

Not every ethical breach is subject to the broad light of public scrutiny. In many cases, the individual involved in unethical behavior keeps his or her job. However, a reputation is developed. It's not a bright and shining one; it's tarnished. The individual becomes known as someone more concerned about personal gain than the interests of others.

Finally, and perhaps most importantly, being unethical can erode your very soul. Most successful financial services professionals realize that business is just a part of life; that their work lives cannot be completely separate and apart from their private lives. However, the various aspects of our lives are interwoven; the ethical tenets professionals practice carry over and are a part of both areas of life. A well-grounded value system provides successful individuals with a full ethical professional life and a full ethical life with friends and family. It is a kind of integrity or wholeness that helps the individual live well.

WHY STUDY ETHICS?

There is no guarantee that, through the study of ethics, you will become a better person. But it can help you realize the ethical implications of some behaviors you might not have considered, and it can give you a systematic tool for dealing with tough ethical situations. A study of ethics increases your awareness of the principled reasons behind your judgments as well as the direct consequences and indirect implications of your actions.

Sometimes people simply don't realize that what they are doing is ethically problematic. We all know what happens when a financial services trainee comes under the direction of an unscrupulous trainer, whose only thought is to make money. The trainee starts to think that coercive salesmanship is the norm in the industry. "Everyone acts that way" becomes a rationalization used to justify unacceptable behavior. Sometimes, people need to be taught the right way to do things. Sometimes, people without experience have just never thought about certain activities as being unethical. People often need tools to help resolve a difficult situation. Ideally, the study of ethics can help in these areas.

ETHICS AS A SET OF BELIEFS ABOUT WHAT IS RIGHT AND WRONG

No person grows up isolated from some group or society, or that person would not survive. We all inherit our attitudes and beliefs about right and wrong from the groups that nurtured us. We learn ethical rules when we are young, and the rules can become so internalized that we rarely think about them; they become almost second nature to us. If we think of our mind as a kind of file cabinet in which these rules and ethical beliefs are stored, with a little effort we can take inventory of our beliefs. For example, a person might believe euthanasia is wrong, capital punishment is wrong, lying is wrong, and so on. The list of beliefs and attitudes concerning actions and social practices can go on indefinitely.

Those attitudes and beliefs come from many areas of society—family, religion, school, TV, peers, the workplace, and so on. While some learn their attitudes and beliefs from the Ten Commandments, their parents, or their church or synagogue, it is possible in this day and age that just as many people learn their rules from television. Think of all the rules of sharing and of being kind and considerate that a child learns from Sesame Street or from the TV characters Barney and Sponge Bob, where it is always clear who is good and who is bad. No matter where the rules are learned or how they are learned, these attitudes and beliefs form a set of ethical or moral rules for behavior.

THE PURPOSE OF ETHICAL RULES

One of the primary purposes of ethical rules is to help society function smoothly so people can get along and flourish together, rather than to fight and destroy each other. Society is a web of relationships, and a well-functioning society is based on healthy relationships. Hence, the purpose of morality and ethics is to help relationships that are healthy to not only to survive, but also to flourish.

According to Stanley Cavell, morality is a "social institution (and/or God-given set of laws), composed of a set of standards about practices, defining right or wrong, for the purpose of rationally adjudicating disputes while allowing relationships to continue."[22] This definition is crucial, for it points out why we have ethics—to help settle disputes while preserving relationships that are necessary for the society's wellbeing. There are, of course, unethical ways of settling disputes. For example, we can settle disputes by using brute power or force; but if we do that, we fall into the law of the jungle, where might makes right.

Human beings do not have to revert to the use of pure force to settle disputes. People have the ability to use reason, to figure out the ways to resolve their disputes and maintain relationships. Reason helps in the development of ethical or moral codes. For example, our reason tells us that, if we don't share some things, life will be "nasty, brutish, and short," as the 17th century English philosopher Thomas Hobbes put it. So we teach our children to share and to be fair at a very early age. We recommend that they don't fight over a toy, and we show them that it will be much better if they take turns and cooperate. When we get older and more sophisticated, we recommend to our colleagues that they seek win-win situations.

Our attitudes about who has a right to what, and who deserves what, reflect our ethical beliefs and give us ways to resolve disputes while allowing relationships to flourish. Human beings dialogue, negotiate, and attempt to reach agreement about what's just or fair. Those agreed-upon beliefs, which are the means for resolving their disputes, comprise their ethics or morality. If we never had disputes, we might not need ethics because we could all just do what we wished. But we don't have everything we wish or need, and we do have disputes, so we do need ethics.

---

22.   Stanley Cavell. (1980) "The Claims of Reason." New York: Oxford University Press: 245.

If ethics is a social enterprise used for resolving disputes, it follows that it is a mistake to think of ethics as a purely subjective or personal matter. As we have seen, the main purpose of ethics is the resolution of interpersonal disputes in which the individual is only one player among many. We are not the source of our ethical beliefs, and the purpose of ethics is not to help us achieve what we want. Such a view is frightfully egocentric. Most of our beliefs came from outside us and were impressed on us by members of the culture into which we were born.

We can, of course, reflect on our beliefs to see if we should submit to being governed by them. It is when we become reflective about these beliefs that we enter the domain of philosophizing about ethics, but the beliefs are there long before we begin such reflection. In that sense, we have ethics (our set of beliefs and attitudes) before we practice good ethics (reflect on and evaluate our beliefs and attitudes). The answer to the question of whether or not we should submit to the rule of our beliefs is not determined by whether or not we want to submit to them, but by our examination of their purpose and whether that purpose is justifiable.

EVALUATING OUR ETHICAL BELIEFS

At some time in our lives, our moral beliefs will either conflict with each other or be challenged. The challenge will arise from experiencing harsh reality or from someone who holds an opposing opinion or lives in a different group or society with a somewhat different set of rules. At that point, a cognitive/affective disequilibrium will occur and we will have to reflect on the adequacy of one or more of our beliefs. It is then that we begin to practice ethics—the philosophical discipline—through the analysis and evaluation of our ethical beliefs.

For example, Huck Finn grew up believing slavery was okay, that slaves were the property of their masters, and that runaway slaves needed to be returned to their masters. Huck's beliefs were challenged when he traveled down the Mississippi with Jim, the runaway slave. Jim looked as human to Huck as any other man. So Huck began to question the ethical rules with which he grew up. How was it right to treat two people who are the same so differently? Huck confronted the issue of justice. He ran up against the principle that, if two people are the same, they should be treated the same. We all go through such epiphanies when our values or moral beliefs are challenged. We either ignore the challenge or do ethics. That is, we begin to analyze what we believe and then evaluate whether those beliefs are adequate.

As we mentioned before, it is possible that a young financial services professional would fall under the spell of an unscrupulous mentor who teaches her exploitative sales techniques and then justifies them by saying, "That's the way we do it in this business. Just make the numbers." The ethical professional will smell something wrong in such a situation and try to get out of it. That's what happened at Health South, where older financial officers (many of whom were convicted of fraud) told their younger counterparts to falsify financial statements, because "that's the way things are done in the real world."

Ethics cannot be avoided, even if we wanted to. One of the most popular phenomena of today is talk radio, and more particularly, sports talk radio. But after talking about who is the better baseball or basketball player, the talk often moves on to ethical issues. Should a pro football team renegotiate a contract? Should a steroid user be let into the Hall of Fame? Should a basketball player be suspended for violating a league drug policy? Should players honor their contracts? Do players have a duty to be role models? The answer to any of these questions requires that a person has a set of beliefs about what's fair or just, what's appropriate or inappropriate, what's good and what's bad—a set of beliefs he or she uses to adjudicate disputes. In short, the answer to any of these questions requires having an ethic and doing ethics.

Doing ethics is engaging in philosophical speculation about how we ought to live. In its most academic form, ethics is that branch of philosophy concerned with analyzing, explaining, and/or justifying the rules of right and wrong. The part of ethics that analyzes and evaluates is reflective. It reflects on our learned customs and mores to judge what they demand of us or others and whether those demands are sufficient or appropriate.

Take a simple example of rules being subject to various interpretations. Does the commandment "Thou shalt not kill" simply prohibit killing human beings, or does it extend to animals and plants? Albert Schweitzer thought it referred to all living creatures. Does it even extend to all humans? Are there exceptions? Defenders of capital punishment argue that it does not apply to all humans. Do other animals have rights? To answer these questions, we must engage in ethical analysis.

Causes for Ethical Reflection

Three situations that cause ethical reflection:

- when the standards or rules we were taught are not clear and hence may be subject to various interpretations
- when those standards or rules conflict with one another
- when those standards or rules conflict with the standards or rules of other groups

What about situations in which standards or rules conflict with one another? Suppose the obligations of family life conflict with those of work. Suppose your obligation to your company conflicts with your obligation to your client. How do you resolve those conflicts?

Finally, consider situations in which our rules and standards conflict with those of other people. Think of the conflicts over abortion, euthanasia or capital punishment in our society. Consider the conflicts over the proper way to treat women in various cultures. Or, closer to our immediate concerns, consider the conflict over the acceptability of rebates or disclosure of commissions in the field of life insurance. Are there ways to resolve these disputes?

FOUR BASIC ETHICAL BELIEFS

To solve ethical disputes, we need to make judgments about alternative courses of action. We make such judgments by investigating the reasons why some actions are deemed ethically appropriate and others are not. For example, we should not falsify an application because that is a lie. We could ask, "Why is lying wrong?" And we would get a host of answers: "Lies hurt people." "Lies use other people." "To lie is not to play fair."

There are a number of reasons why we approve or disapprove of our actions. One basic reason why we approve of an action is that the action is beneficial. We disapprove of actions that are harmful. This provides us with a basic ethical principle: "Do good and avoid harm." A second reason why we approve of an action is that it is just or fair. Fairness concerns lead us to the principle of respect for others: "Do unto others as you would have them do unto you"—the Golden Rule. A third reason why an action should be carried out is that a person has promised to do it. This reflects the principle, "Keep your word." Finally, actions are acceptable because they allow people to keep their integrity. This exemplifies the principle, "Be true to yourself."

On a practical level, ethics attempts to apply these four ethical principles to specific situations. Sometimes situations are complicated and the principles conflict—for example, when keeping a promise will do harm or breaking a promise will bring about some good. There are actions in which the principles conflict with beneficial consequences, or when fairness leads to undesirable consequences. We will deal with those cases later. For now, let us note that the principles give us sound guidance about how to act.

These principles give us a clear set of reasons that ethically justify actions. Let's review the reasons. If the action benefits me or society, that is a good reason to do it. If the action harms me or society, that is a good reason not to do it. If I promised to perform the action, that is a good reason to do it, unless it is somehow harmful to me or society. If it is unfair or unjust, that is a good reason not to do it. If the action violates someone's rights, that is a good reason not to do it. Remember: Ethical issues or problems arise only when there are good reasons to perform and good reasons not to perform actions. We can summarize these four reasons in an acronym which we called the **GIFT**. **G** is for the goodness of the action. **I** is for the Integrity of the action. **F** is for the fairness of the action and **T** is for the trustworthiness of the person who promises to perform a certain action. At some time in our lives, our moral beliefs will either conflict with each other or be challenged. The challenge will arise from experiencing harsh reality or from someone who holds an opposing opinion or lives in a different group or society with a somewhat different set of rules. At that point, a cognitive/affective disequilibrium will occur and we will have to reflect on the adequacy of one or more of our beliefs. It is then that we begin to do ethics—the philosophical discipline—through the analysis and evaluation of our ethical beliefs.

Basic Ethical Principles: The GIFT©
• **Goodness** (Do good and avoid harm.)
• **Integrity.** (Be true to yourself)
• **Fairness** (Be fair).
• **Trustworthiness** (Keep your word.)

SIX QUESTIONS TO ASCERTAIN THE ETHICS OF AN ACTION

To ascertain whether there are good reasons for an action, such as those mentioned above, there is a set of questions which depend upon those reasons. We can expand the GIFT and come up with six important questions to ask in order to determine the ethical probity of any action.

Is the Action Good for Me?

In judging an action, one should always ask, "Will it hurt or help me?" Obviously, if an action is beneficial to the person performing the action, that is a good reason for that person to do it. For example, a very important reason to work is that work is beneficial because it provides the wherewithal to live and, ideally, it allows a person to engage in fulfilling activity. Meaningful work is work that is beneficial to the person. We have a need to be creative and productive, and meaningful work can help us fulfill that need. Hence, it is good for us.

In the earlier scenario about joining a service club, it was illustrated that some people are suspicious of self-interested motivation and are, therefore, hesitant to defend actions that are beneficial to themselves. That is a mistake. Healthy self-interest is a good thing.

Remember that in the New Testament one of the commandments is to love your neighbor as yourself. We take that to mean, that if you don't love yourself and look out for yourself, you should not apply the Golden Rule. If you do not concern yourself with your own benefit, who will? Still, it is necessary to make some distinctions here.

One needs to look out for oneself, but there are limits on that. Self-interest is a good thing, but selfishness is not. It is unethical to be selfish. But we should recognize that selfishness is not the equivalent of looking out for one's own interest. It is looking out for one's own interest at the expense of another. So, be self-interested, but not selfish.

A second distinction needs to be made between what we want or desire and what is good for us. What we want and desire is not necessarily beneficial to us. Our wants and our desires are a mixed bag. I want the piece of pie, but it is not good for me because I am on a diet. Because of the distinction between wants and needs, we should get clear about what counts as "good."

For our purposes, let's define the "good" for human beings as that which fulfills basic human needs. There are obviously things that are good for trees and animals and the environment, but we need not concern ourselves with those goods. Human beings have different levels of need. There are physical needs for food, shelter, and clothing. There is the need for health and some minimum wealth, enough to purchase those necessities. Beyond that, because human beings are social, there are needs for fulfilling their social dimension, such as the need for early training in how to get along in society, as well as the need to relate to other people—as in friendship. Finally, because human beings are potential producers, they need to be active and creative. Hence, there is a dimension within human beings that needs meaningful activity. Humans need projects and goals and actions with a point to them. These are the needs that fulfill the creative level. Providing these needs for oneself is an important reason for performing an action. Thus, in some cases, we can justify our belief that an action is good, simply by showing that it is good for us, insofar as it fulfills one or more of our needs. Any number of philosophers call that fulfillment happiness, which can get translated into living well and fulfilling our potential.

Is the Action Good for Others?

A second question to ask of any action is whether it is good or beneficial for others. When we think ethically, we do not stop at considering the benefit of the action for ourselves; we go further and think of its benefits for everyone affected. Not every action performed in the world affects us directly, although certain actions have a wider impact than the agent may originally suspect. For example, an act of fraud may contribute to increased regulatory and compliance burdens. These additional costs to the company may be passed on to consumers in terms of higher prices and to employees in terms of lower wages. However, it is evident that an action can be wrong, whether or not it affects me. Simply, if a good reason for doing an action is that it benefits us, and if everyone counts as much as we do, then usually the more people benefit that from an action, the better the action. Of course, our desire to promote the good of as many people as possible must be tempered with a recognition that at times the good of the majority can come at the expense of the rights and goods of the minority. (Note that the questions about benefit or harm deal with the consequences of the action. The next set of questions deals more with the action itself.)

Is the Action Fair or Just?

Fairness rests on the principle of identity. It is only logical to believe that if two things are the same, they should be treated in the same way. How can you justify treating one person differently from another if there are no relevant differences between them? Of course, someone might have two identical people in need and only enough goods for one of them. In that situation, we would not know to whom to give the goods. In such a case, flipping a coin is as fair a solution as any. Consider the following: If there is no relevant difference between two children, they are both being given a piece of cake, and there is enough cake to go around, shouldn't they each get a piece of roughly the same size? One cannot justify giving one child or the other a larger piece. However, if it were one of the children's birthdays, then the children are not the same in all relevant respects, and it would be fair to give a larger piece to the birthday child since the fact that it is one person's birthday, and we do special things for people on their birthdays, creates a good relevant reason for the birthday child to get a bigger piece of cake.

The principle of justice or fairness, which is in many ways the basis of ethical thinking and puts limits on the pursuit of self-interest, holds that "the same should be treated the same." We all recognize and use this principle. To see that, you need only to reflect on how annoyed you get when someone, who you think is no better than you are, gets special treatment. You think that person does not deserve it any more than you do. Thus, if an action treats people unfairly—that is, differently, without a good reason—it is ethically suspect.

Is There a Commitment to Perform the Action?

A fourth important question to ask has to do with trustworthiness. Can you trust someone to keep their promises? We need to ask: "Is there a commitment?" Were any promises made to do something? If there were, they ought to be kept.

Keeping promises is a good reason for doing something. We need to note that there are commitments that go beyond those that result from explicit promises and contracts. Any lasting relationship rests on implied promises and expectations of guaranteed behavior in spite of the contingencies of the future. Customers expect to get the benefits promised in insurance advertisements and do not expect to be cheated because of disclaimers in the small print. A professor commits himself or herself to show up for a class a certain number of times, at a certain time, and for a certain length of time.

Our commitments were made in the past, penetrate the future and bind us to a course of action, no matter whether we feel like keeping our promises or not. Human beings are unique promise-making animals. Although other species act largely by instinct, human beings set up their relationships with each other on the basis of expectations and promises. Hence, we can say that the basis of any ethics is to keep one's commitments. It is one of the things that distinguishes us from the rest of the animal kingdom. Our social structure depends on promises and cannot function if these promises are not kept. Thus, another very good reason for doing something is that you have made a promise or commitment.

Does the Action Preserve My Integrity?

This question is related to the previous one. If people keep their commitments, they are true to their word. In one sense, someone's word defines a person. Our promises and commitments define what we are, and failure to keep them makes us irresponsible and unfaithful to our word. Keeping one's word is as much a part of integrity as being honest. But there is another aspect of integrity. The word integrity comes from the field of integers in mathematics. Integers are whole numbers. Integrity, therefore, means "wholeness." A person who acts one way in business and another in his or her personal life lacks integrity. A business decision that is not in conformity with personal values fractures a person and can destroy his or her integrity. The notion that the only point of business is to make money or a profit, is a notion that can fracture a business. Consider what one would do if there were a choice between being ethical or making a large commission. How many people are tempted to lie to make money? To do that is to lack integrity. We have to put the profit motive and the making money motive in their appropriate places so that we are not torn between money and ethics. That is why integrity is important.

Is the Action Legal?

This is the final question to ask when evaluating an action: "Is it legal?" Assuming that laws are in conformity with what is ethical and beneficial to society, it is required that we obey them. Breaking the law can lead to punishment, but where the laws are good and beneficial, breaking them also leads to the undermining of the societal order. All financial services professionals are familiar with the many regulations and laws that govern their practice and the burden of compliance imposed on them. Ethics and the law are not identical, and there can be unjust laws. Since the relation of the law to ethics is so complicated, we will defer an examination of it to another chapter.

Ethical Decision Procedure
Six questions to ask when evaluating an action or practice from an ethical point of view: • *An answer of "yes" to all means we have an unqualifiedly good action or practice*   • *An answer of "no" to all means we have an unqualifiedly bad action or practice.*   • *"Yes" and "no" answers mean we have a complicated ethical issue that needs sophisticated analysis. Follow these points*   1. Does it benefit me?   2. Does it benefit all the others affected by the action?   3. Is it fair?   4. Does it meet my commitments?   5. Does it preserve my integrity?   6. Is it legal?

A DECISION PROCEDURE

By using the preceding questions, we can set up a decision procedure to discover what we should do when faced with an ethical dilemma. If we answer "yes" to all of the questions, we have an action that clearly should be done, an action we could call unqualifiedly good or right. If we answer "no" to all of them, it is an action that should not be done, one unqualifiedly bad or wrong. If we are thinking of selling a financial product that brings a profit to the company, a commission to us, benefits others, and doesn't in the process treat anyone unfairly or violate some promise or commitment, because there are nothing but good reasons for doing it, it should be done. However, if I am tempted to fraudulently sell off defective products, and I see that it is not beneficial to me, the company (because we will be sued), its executives, or the general society, then that action would be deceptive and, hence, unfair. It would also violate the relationship of trust that we have with the community. In this case, all the answers are "no," and there is every reason for not performing the action.

This is a procedure for deciding what to do and what not to do. If an action benefits you and others, does not violate fairness or a commitment, and preserves my integrity, it should be done. If, on the other hand, an action does not benefit you or others, is unfair, requires breaking a commitment, or violates my integrity, it should not be done. If we get mixed answers of "yes" and "no" (if, for example, the action benefits society but is unfair or vice versa), then we are faced with an ethical dilemma. Ethical dilemmas are difficult, sometimes impossible, to resolve because, in a sense, we are "damned if you do and damned if you don't." These are the gray areas of ethical decisionmaking that take hard thought and moral imagination to work our way through a true ethical dilemma.

ROLE MORALITY

In the area of financial services, trust and promise keeping are essential for the true professional. We will talk about the nature of the professional in a later chapter, but for now we want to talk about the importance of keeping promises. Keeping promises is at the basis of what is called role morality. It might be that the best way to do well and to avoid harm while being fair is to honor one's commitments. We have seen that ethics, largely the product of society, allows a society to flourish. One of the ways in which society flourishes is by cooperation, which requires the building of relationships and the division of labor. We get along because we have rules and relationships, which give each person in society a set of responsibilities. The growth of market economics has made the delivery of financial services an essential factor in developing a flourishing society. Hence, society, as it has developed, needs the services of the financial planner and advisor.

Review Item: What do I do here?

Agency Manager: Pete, you need to make some sales to meet your production quotas. Why not push some of these variable annuities? If you don't get moving we're going to have to terminate your contract with the company.

Joe Producer: I do have a few elderly clients who could use some annuities. They have some hefty surrender charges, but the clients probably don't need the liquidity. I'll give them a call.

Is Joe thinking ethically here? What would you suggest?

The fact that you decided to enter the field of financial services means you have made a commitment. Financial services professionals have different constituencies with whom they have relationships and, consequently, toward whom they have responsibilities. Those various constituencies include clients, companies, the profession, yourself, other professionals, and the law. Assuming an important ethical obligation—taken voluntarily—is to do our job, then it is necessary to examine what that job entails, to determine our responsibilities. Doing our job involves servicing clients in a professional way by using products of companies and services of other related professionals under the existing laws. We enter into a relationship with each of these constituencies, which means that we have ethical responsibilities toward each of them. To get a full picture of the financial services professional's ethical responsibilities, we need to look at all the constituencies and what is owed to them.

There are six major constituencies to which the financial services professional has ethical obligations as a result of relationships that are based on explicit or implicit promises.

ETHICAL OBLIGATIONS TO SIX CONSTITUENCIES

Obligations to the Client

Generally, the obligation to put the client's interest first is seen as the primary responsibility of the financial services professional. We will examine issues of how this is best done and look at specific practices that either fulfill or undermine these obligations.

Obligations to the Company

Each individual agent or service provider operates, to some extent, as an agent or broker for a company that creates the product being recommended or sold. It is important to look at the various types of relationships that exist between an agent or broker and the company, because they can be quite dissimilar and carry different responsibilities. In chapter 4, we will look at the agency/principal relationship to investigate to what extent truth and loyalty are owed to companies. What are the different obligations for a captive agent and an independent agent. To whom do brokers owe loyalty?

Obligations to the Profession

We, as financial services professionals, are by our very name designated as professionals. That means we possess specialized knowledge and operate in a position of trust. We should conduct our practices according to a professional code. In chapter 5 we will look at what is involved in being a professional as well as what the various codes typically require. Professional status can be a two-edged sword: With increased recognition comes increased responsibility, and with increased responsibility comes increased liability.

Obligations to Allied Professionals

Given the increased complexity of financial products, it is necessary for planners and advisors to depend on people from allied professions, such as law and accounting, to give proper advice to clients. As a result of this dependence, and a multidisciplinary approach to financial services, some ethical difficulties arise.

Obligations to Ourselves and Others Related to Us

A sometimes overlooked obligation is the obligation to oneself. We sometimes think it is okay to do what we want with our lives; at the same time we condemn others for wasting their talents. We each have an obligation to ourselves to create a worthwhile life of integrity. As John Donne said, "No man is an island." We live with others and, consequently, have responsibilities toward them. We are extremely close to some of those people, such as our families, who are often extensions of our own ego. We often hear a person justify making a problematic sale as doing it not for himself or herself, but for his or her family.

Obligations to Society and Its Laws

Financial services professionals are an essential part of society. Society needs them and, to make sure its needs are well met, has established laws and regulations to help achieve those needs. Financial services professionals are regulated by both the federal and state governments. Although this course cannot examine all the regulations in every state, we will cover key elements of regulations that have a commonality from state to state and are demanded by the federal government. Knowledge of the various laws is important. It helps financial services professionals to stay out of trouble and avoid the heavy penalties that can be applied for violations. These penalties can include license suspension or revocation—the type of penalties that can end a career. (We will look at the requirements of the law in the next chapter.)

Those to Whom We Have Obligations
• the client
• the company
• the profession
• other allied professionals
• ourselves and others related to us
• the laws

SUMMARY

From a societal point of view, we can probably reduce most of ethics to keeping one's commitments. Ethics are a reflection of the rules of behavior we have learned from our society to help us determine what we ought to do and how we ought to live. These rules constitute our everyday knowledge of what's right and wrong. If we are to take control of our own lives, we must reflect on those rules, accept or reject them, then either make them our own or replace them with other rules. Socrates claimed that the unexamined life is not worth living. Examination requires reflection on the rules of behavior. This reflection, which involves analysis and evaluation of these rules, constitutes doing ethics and is part of this course.

CHAPTER REVIEW QUESTIONS

Answers to Review Questions are found in the Appendix.

1. Which of the following best describes the term "ethics?"

    (A) Ethics asks what should be done in a given situation.
    (B) Ethics deals with what is done in a given situation.
    (C) Ethics is the process of planning philanthropy.
    (D) Ethics means living in a self-interested manner.

2. What is the purpose of rules?

    (A) to control the lives of citizens
    (B) to make society an orderly place
    (C) to reveal who are the followers and who are the leaders
    (D) to create conformity to a standard of behavior

3. According to Stanley Cavel, a "social institution (and/or God-given set of laws) composed of a set of standards about practices, defining right or wrong, for the purpose of rationally adjudicating disputes while allowing relationships to continue" is called

    (A) rules
    (B) ethics
    (C) love
    (D) morality

4. What is the essential message in the Golden Rule?

    (A) You shall not commit adultery.
    (B) One is motivated by an inner drive to improve the quality of life.
    (C) The pursuit of one's interest is at the expense of another.
    (D) Do unto others as you would have them do unto you.

5. Adam Smith in "The Wealth of Nations" provided us with an ethical framework for modern business that is often called the

    (A) Golden Rule model
    (B) enlightened self-interest model
    (C) planned philanthropy model
    (D) utilitarian model

READ THE FOLLOWING DIRECTIONS BEFORE CONTINUING

The questions below differ from the preceding questions in that they all contain the word EXCEPT. So you understand fully the basis used in selecting each answer, be sure to read each question carefully.

6.   All of the following statements concerning morals are correct EXCEPT

   (A)   All cultures have the same basic moral principles.
   (B)   Any adult of any group comes equipped with a set of moral or ethical rules in his or her head that he or she "inherited" from his or her culture.
   (C)   In some cases, moral codes are developed in conjunction with religious beliefs.
   (D)   In some cases, moral codes are developed as a result of customs founded to promote human harmony.

7.   The text states that ethics is essential to business for all of the following reasons EXCEPT

   (A)   If there were no ethics in business, there would be no trust.
   (B)   If there were no ethics in business, no one would keep promises.
   (C)   If there were no ethics in business, there would be no lawsuits.
   (D)   If there were no ethics in business, there would be no reliability.

8.   All of the following are situations which cause ethical reflection EXCEPT

   (A)   when the standards or rules we were taught are not clear and subject to interpretation
   (B)   when the rules and standards have been accepted by all those around us
   (C)   when the rules or standards conflict with one another
   (D)   when those standards or rules conflict with those of other groups of people

9.   All of the following are general ethical principals EXCEPT

   (A)   Be fair.
   (B)   Keep your word.
   (C)   Be true to yourself.
   (D)   Always have goals.

10.   All of the following are major constituencies to whom the financial services professional has an ethical obligation EXCEPT

      (A)   the client
      (B)   the company
      (C)   the law
      (D)   the family

<table>
<tr><th colspan="2">Learning Objectives</th></tr>
<tr><td colspan="2">An understanding of the material in this chapter should enable the student to</td></tr>
</table>

Learning Objectives

An understanding of the material in this chapter should enable the student to

1. Define the relationship between law and ethics.

2. Describe the distinction between compliance and ethics.

3. Identify state and federal regulations governing financial services professionals.

THE LAW AND ETHICS

There is a false dichotomy between ethics and the law that is expressed by the cliché, "You can't legislate morality." Clearly, this is not universally true. We legislate morality all the time, and if we reflect for only a few moments, we can see how law and ethics are intertwined. Every community of any size needs to have customs which tell the individual members how to behave. Otherwise, the community would be disorderly. When members are born into that community, they are taught the rules. They become socialized into the community. For a society to survive, there will be rules against lying, cheating, killing, stealing and other actions we consider unethical actions. However, in time, individuals begin to break some of the rules. So the society codifies the rules and stipulates punishments for those who break the rules. In that way, at some point, governmental units, such as cities or countries, develop laws that prescribe a framework for what the governing unit considers to be minimal standards of conduct that will allow the community to survive and help its citizens flourish. Sanctions are established to discourage people from violating those standards. Thus, law has been described as reasonable ordinances promulgated by legitimate authorities for the sake of the common good.

Some ethical theorists make a distinction between the moral law (which refers to ethical rules) and positive law (which refers to laws of governments). All laws are rules and have a shared goal and a shared origin—the common good. The positive law seems relatively clear to the extent that it is written down. Hence, lawyers, police officers, and court officials who are all employed in the justice system have a body of legislation by which they determine if a law is broken. Of course, there can be disagreements about the interpretation of those written laws. However, even as those interpretations evolve, there is a concrete and accessible legal system in place.

Unlike positive law, the moral law (ethical rules) is not written down. There are commonly accepted rules and standards of behavior regarding the basic rules that govern the moral life. These include such rules as:

- Do not kill.
- Do not deceive.
- Do not cause pain.
- Do not disable.
- Do not cheat.
- Keep your promises.

These injunctions reflect the commonly-held expectations about how people should live in society. They reinforce the importance we place both on the rights and dignity of the individual and our obligations to other people. Some of these rules have corresponding civil laws, while others do not.

But it is not only the government that passes laws to regulate behavior. Rules can be promulgated by a variety of organizations. Industries and specific business organizations develop their own codes of ethical conduct and statements of values, which deal with behavior that the law does not address.

Our shared ethical values provide the rules and standards of conduct that govern us as citizens of a nation, members of an organization, or simply in our individual lives. To the extent that one freely chooses to be a part of a group, culture or organization, one voluntarily accepts the standards of that group, culture or organization.

Because the law is necessarily incomplete, these ethical standards become a higher benchmark against which the organization's conduct is measured. That higher benchmark is often referred to as the "spirit of the law," as contrasted with the "letter of the law," since the "spirit of the law" interprets what the positive law would dictate if it were applied to a specific situation. We can usually understand the "spirit of the law" as the purpose to be served by the law. We have law *x* so that we can bring about purpose *y*. For example, we have tax laws to benefit the common good. Nevertheless, there are tax abuses that might be within the "letter of the law," but violate the spirit.

As we have seen, laws are standards that society has codified in order to enforce certain behaviors. Ethics, via the law and codes, gives us rules and standards of conduct that govern us as citizens of a nation, members of an organization, or simply in our individual/societal lives.

The following diagram illustrates the relationship between law and ethics.

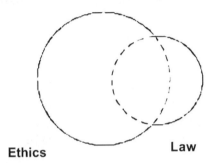

Ethics   **Law**

As shown here, law and ethics overlap, but each also has its own domain. The dotted line at the intersection of law and ethics represents a mutual boundary. As we have seen, laws are standards that society has codified in order to enforce certain behaviors.

BUSINESS LAW AND BUSINESS ETHICS

What holds for the relationship between law and ethics also holds for business ethics with business law. Business ethics and business law overlap regarding such issues as the fulfillment of contractual agreements, laws against fraud, agency law, contract law, liability law, labor law, and employee rights law—including nondiscriminatory treatment of different racial groups in hiring and promotion decisions and meeting minimal quality-control and safety standards in manufacturing processes.

Within the realm of business ethics (but outside the realm of business law) are areas either not covered or insufficiently covered by existing laws (such as layoffs, downsizing, and marketing practices, which are manipulative but not fraudulent), as well as concerns (such as the acceptable level of toxic waste emitted or dumped into the environment), regarding companies' knowledge of inadequate or nonexistent legal standards. Other examples include verbal abuse in the workplace, sales practices, and intimidation of subordinates.

Business law outside the ethical domain may include trade regulations, product specifications and contractual relationships with suppliers, customers, the community, shareholders and investors. However, many "purely legal" rules quickly become ethical issues if they are violated, intentionally misinterpreted or ignored. If a law or regulation is passed to serve the common good, then it would usually be unethical to violate that law. In fact, as we have seen, laws represent codified ethical standards. The positive laws are the minimum moral requirements that we have agreed to demand for society as a whole.

Law and ethics, working in harmony, are essential for any civilization to continue and neither is sufficient unto itself. Both are social institutions, developed to help civilization survive (and what is true for society at large is true for business in general and the financial services industry in particular).

Let's examine this relationship in the area of financial services. We begin by looking at the purposes, which are twofold. The first purpose of financial services is to provide security for clients by working to mitigate the harm caused by an unexpected and unmanageable financial loss. The second purpose is to produce a financial gain for clients. It is obvious that these purposes are often combined in the objectives and expectations of an individual client. Given these objectives, financial institutions were created to serve the public. Thus, the spirit of the law requires financial services professionals to work to serve the interests and needs of the client.

In many cases, the law simply sets minimum requirements for behavior. It does not set optimum standards for acting as a professional. If you follow the requirements of the law as a financial services professional, you have started on the path to ethical behavior. If you act without regard for the law, you could be acting unethically and may invite professional ruin. Acting within the parameters of the law immediately adds credibility to actions undertaken by the financial services professional. But let's look more carefully at the relationship between ethics and compliance.

COMPLIANCE AND ETHICS

George Washington, Benjamin Franklin, Thomas Jefferson and the other founding fathers of the United States were not inclined to comply with the law unless they had good reasons to do so. Those reasons were not provided by authoritarian declarations, but by appeals to sound ethical principles. As we learned from the American Revolution, a demand for compliance without accompanying good reasons can create resentment.

Compliance has its good side. It is necessary when the internal controls or mores that provide for an orderly and just society have lost their effect.

As we have seen, when ethical expectations are not met, society calls upon legal remedies, which, unlike appeals to morality, can impose civil and criminal sanctions that penalize undesirable behavior.

As we know all too well, breakdowns in ethical behavior on the part of some members of the insurance and financial services industry required the introduction of legal remedies, the end result of which was the emphasis (some would say overemphasis) on compliance. While the goal of compliance—to establish or reestablish ethical behavior—is laudable, the resulting new emphasis on compliance and compliance training leaves a lot to be desired.

COMPLIANCE NEEDS ETHICS

Even though the goal of compliance is to help improve ethical behavior, simply concerning ourselves with being in compliance and satisfying the letter of the law will not improve ethical behavior by itself; being in compliance with the law is not the equivalent of being ethical. To equate following the law with being ethical is a mistaken view.

To illustrate how being ethical demands that we go beyond the law, let's review one of the great moral stories of Western culture—the story of the good Samaritan. A man traveling the road from Jerusalem to Jericho is attacked by robbers and left to die on the side of the road. A priest and Levite pass the man by, and it is only a Samaritan—the supposed enemy of the man—who stops to help him. It is clear that when the priest and the Levite passed by the wounded man, they did nothing illegal. But there has been near universal agreement that the priest and Levite were morally irresponsible and that the real moral hero is the Samaritan who, in spite of his fear and hatred of Jews in the abstract, was led by sympathy for his wounded fellow man. Therefore, although a legal evaluation of the priest and Levite would find nothing illegal, a moral evaluation would find them morally deficient. This story reveals why going beyond the law is morally required. Ethics calls on us to do more than just obey the law.

Clarence Walton, the first chairholder in ethics at The American College, posits a Law of Social Motivation which asserts "...that in advanced industrial affluent and democratic societies, people demand that consideration of the common welfare be borne in mind by large private associations—even when the law is silent on such demands." In short, neither individuals nor companies meet their full ethical responsibilities when they simply aim to stay in compliance.

COMPLIANCE AND THE LETTER OF THE LAW

Because compliance is targeted at meeting the basic legal requirements, it emphasizes the letter of the law, rather than addressing the reasons for the law or the spirit of the law. But just as an arrow aimed too low will miss the target, aiming only to meet the basic requirements of compliance—to be in accord with the letter of the law—will fail to hit the target of acting ethically (that is, acting in the spirit of the law).

Simply meeting the demands of compliance does not always make it ethical. For example, consider your disgust when, upon purchasing a product on the strength of an advertisement, you discover you are not getting nearly the bargain you had thought you were getting because you had not read the ad's small print. Although the small print in the advertisement meets the legal requirements and puts the company in compliance, it manipulates the customer and fails to live up to the spirit of the law against false advertising.

The spirit of any law for truth in advertising rests on a moral belief that a prospective customer has a right to know what he or she is purchasing (informed consent) and should be able to make that choice freely, without being manipulated. If the small print is there merely so a company can be in compliance, then being in compliance violates the spirit of the law. Thus, by aiming only at being in compliance, we may end up being unethical.

ACTING TO AVOID PUNISHMENT

There are two reasons for obeying the law or being ethical. First, it is the right thing to do. Second, we do not want to get caught and be punished. We often do things because we wish to avoid penalties and punishment. Fear is a very effective motivating tool. Consider what happens, however, when fear of punishment or avoidance of penalties becomes the only reason for acting. If the sole motive for acting in a particular way in certain circumstances is to avoid punishment, then when punishments to avoid in those circumstances no longer exist, the reason for acting in that way is removed. If your only reason for not lying is that you are afraid of the consequences of getting caught, what reason do you have to avoid lying if you know you will not get caught?

Of course, when an unethical action is declared illegal and a sanction is attached to it, there is an additional motive for not acting in that way. Nonetheless, the primary reason for not acting unethically is that the action hurts people or is unfair. Excessive or exclusive reliance on compliance to motivate ethical activity puts the cart before the horse, and attempting to modify behavior through fear of sanctions sends the wrong message about why it is unacceptable to treat customers or clients unethically.

COMPLIANCE AS REACTIVE RATHER THAN PROACTIVE

There are those who say sports are a microcosm of life. We think this is correct, at least to the extent that we can learn many lessons about life by observing sports behavior. Assume it is Sunday afternoon and you are watching your favorite NFL team. It is the last quarter of the game. Your team has just scored to go ahead by two points and kicks off to the opposition. Your team goes into a prevent defense. Most of the time it doesn't seem to work. Compliance can be likened to a prevent defense that causes the players to sit back on their heels—to react instead of attack.

It is important to make sure that the compliance mentality permeating the financial services industry is not like a prevent defense. This shows us that acting out of defensiveness or fear is rarely as effective as acting in a more proactive and positive way. Acting defensively, with only compliance as our guide, is being reactive, not proactive. Proactive people and companies are robust and confident, they surge forward and are not afraid to make a mistake. Reactive people and companies are retiring and defensive, moving ever so slowly, preferring to do nothing in order to avoid making a mistake.

A company for which decisions are always constrained by a legalistic, hypercautious approach and focuses its sole concern on the avoidance of trouble is a company that has lost its self-confidence. Not much new and creative will come from that company. The paradox is that if your only goal is to protect yourself, you probably won't. Rather, you will create many other problems. There is something disconcerting about a multibillion-dollar corporation that deals with its problems in a dictatorial way when the environment calls for a values-based empowerment approach that builds upon integrity and honesty. With such a culture, a company can be more aggressive and build flexibility into the system. The company's focus must be on what its customers want and how to gear the company toward meeting those needs, instead of focusing on how to avoid litigation.

It is quite popular these days for companies to stress the procedural side of ethics through compliance. It is important, however, that companies begin to look beyond the mere procedural approach and begin building an ethics-based culture throughout the organization for the future that will rely less and less upon compliance. Successful companies do not prosper at the expense of customers; they prosper because of the value they bring to their customers. If a company has a soul, the surest way to lose it is to view the customer as someone to exploit, rather than as someone to serve.

THE DANGER OF A COMPLIANCE BASED MENTALITY

In the current regulatory environment, it is not unusual that many practitioners elide ethics with compliance. But compliance with laws and regulations is not enough to ensure that we are meeting our ethical obligations. This analysis can be helpfully applied at the level of the organization as well as at the individual level. Beyond an analysis of the obligations of individual financial services practitioners, it is important to look at the cultures of the organizations in which we work. It is clear that culture is very important in determining whether individuals act ethically.

An ethical culture cannot simply be defined as one in which there is 'more' emphasis on compliance, although this may certainly be a component of an ethical culture. As Christopher Michelson points out, the difference between ethics and compliance is not necessarily doing 'more' but doing better or doing differently.[23] He makes the important point that ethical behavior is about *choice*. Specifically ethical behavior is about freely intending what is good.

---

23. Michaelson. Christopher (2006) "Compliance and the Illusion of Ethical Progress" Journal of Business Ethics 66: 241

You may have heard the adage that "ethics is what you do when no one is looking." The idea is that an ethical person acts well even when there is no clear reward or punishment for doing so. It is this difference that gets at the heart of the distinction between compliance and ethics, namely, that there is a powerful external motivation and incentive to follow legal rules and regulations, especially in the financial services industry. Compliance violations not only threaten the career and professional prospects of the financial services practitioner, but also have serious financial consequences for an agent and his or her family and may even result in criminal charges. Michelson's point is that, in the meaningful sense of choice, we do not really choose to follow the law.

Consider the example of a man who is held-up at knife point by a criminal who demands that he turn over his wallet and his watch or he will kill him. Now, imagine that several hours later the knife man is apprehended by local police. When he is questioned by the police, he pleads that this is all quite unfair. "He gave me his wallet," the thief says, "I gave him a choice! He did not have to give it to me." Not many police officers (or victims) would be convinced by the thief's justifications and for good reason since we recognize that a choice made while being threatened with bodily harm is not much of a choice. It is possible to develop a continuum of degrees of choice, with one end representing being physically compelled to act and the other end representing a fully free and informed choice.

It is the danger of compelling what could and should be freely given that renders the compliance-driven culture so dangerous and makes the creation of an ethically minded culture so important.

LAWS AND REGULATIONS THAT GOVERN THE INSURANCE INDUSTRY

State Role in Insurance Regulation

The major responsibility for regulation of the insurance industry rests with state governments and is carried out by state insurance departments. State judicial departments act as a primary source of common law rules governing the insurance industry and these responsibilities include monitoring the ethical conduct of licensed agents. These departments regulate insurance in three primary areas:

1. company authorization

2. sales practices
3. company licensing

Company Authorization

State insurance departments determine the companies that are eligible to do business within their borders. Factors taken into consideration in granting this authorization include financial stability and adherence to state laws. Once a company has been authorized to do business within a state, it must also seek approval for each product it wishes to sell within that state. This approval must be obtained before consumers may be approached regarding the product's purchase.

Sales Practices

All states have rules regarding how insurance may be sold. Typically, those rules cover the issues of product misrepresentation, replacement and rebating. For example, presenting insurance as a retirement annuity or a mutual fund is a form of impermissible misrepresentation. In a replacement situation, failure to compare a policy that has already been issued to a newly proposed policy is also an area typically of concern to state regulators. Also, paying a client a "commission kickback" is a violation of the sales practice rules in almost every state.

State insurance laws are not uniform, but they do contain common themes. All states, through laws and regulations, establish rules of practice. These rules provide ethical guidelines by spelling out what an agent may or may not do.

Typically, state laws and regulations cover the following matters:

- *Approved Policies*. Agents may sell only policies that have been filed with and approved by state authorities.
- *Misrepresentation*. Agents are forbidden to misrepresent policy terms or coverage.
- *Replacement*. Agents in most states must follow strict guidelines when replacing coverage.
- *Rebating*. Rebating is forbidden in most states.
- *Timeliness*. Agents are required to perform their duties toward clients in a timely manner. This includes, for example, prompt submission of a completed insurance application.

The Concept of Agency Licensing

All states require agents to be licensed or authorized before they can sell insurance within their borders. The sale of policies by unauthorized insurers or agents is illegal. For some agents, this may mean maintaining just one license in the state in which they live and do business. However, today's mobile population requires many agents serve clients in more than one state. As a result, more agents must maintain nonresident licenses and, therefore, have to comply with the rules and regulations of more than one state. Varying continuing education requirements are one example of how differing state rules can affect an agent.

FEDERAL ROLE IN INSURANCE REGULATION

Even though the insurance industry is predominately regulated by the states, the insurance professional will encounter federal regulation in several areas. In particular, it is important to know how federal regulations affect clients.

- Federal rules apply to the area of antitrust regulation. You become aware of this when you attend industry meetings and receive warnings regarding the exchange of company information, such as product pricing.

- Federal rules apply in the area of taxation of insurance companies. This may be an area far removed from a field agent, but federal taxation affects the cost of products. The Internal Revenue Code contains specific provisions that spell out how both mutual and stock carriers are to be taxed, as well as provisions that affect the tax status of products sold by insurance carriers. For example, the Internal Revenue Code provides for the tax-deferred build-up within a life insurance product as well as income tax-free death proceeds. Knowledge of product-related tax provisions is particularly important to the insurance professional. Providing clients with inaccurate information about the tax consequences of various insurance-related transactions can be an invitation to a lawsuit.

- Federal rules apply in the area of labor and pension regulation. Many financial services companies have large pension departments. Many professionals sell qualified retirement plans, which are subject to both internal Revenue Service and Labor Department rules and regulations. The landmark piece of legislation in this regard is the Employee Retirement Income Security Act of 1974 (ERISA). Pension and retirement planning legislation is an evolving area. Agents who practice in this area must stay abreast of up-to-date developments. Running afoul of these rules can subject the insurance agent to broad-based liability.

- Federal securities rules apply to the insurance industry, particularly in regard to the promotion and sale of variable life and annuity products. These products have at their core investment-type sub-accounts, similar to mutual funds. This means there is an oversight by the Securities and Exchange Commission (SEC) that is carried out through the licensing procedures established by the Financial Industry Regulatory Authority[24] (FINRA). We will discuss more about this later, when we look at laws governing investment advisors.

- In recent years, the federal government has shown increased interest in the regulation of the health insurance industry. At the present time, this has resulted in the standardization of Medicare supplemental policies. The design of long-term care insurance has been influenced by indirect health care legislation in the form of federal tax regulations. In the future, federal oversight may affect basic health care policies and access to care provided by health maintenance organizations (HMOs).

- The ACLI and other groups have been pushing for a federal option where a company could have federal regulators governing insurance companies.

WHAT IS AN AGENT?

The NAIC Model Agents and Brokers Licensing Act defines an insurance agent as "...an individual, partnership or corporation appointed by an insurer to solicit applications for a policy of insurance or to negotiate a policy of insurance *on its behalf*." This appointment is usually evidenced by a written and signed contract between the insurance agent and the carrier. As part of the process, the agent must usually be licensed in the state in which the contracts are to be solicited. Under this definition, the professional is an agent for the company.

---

24. FINRA is the successor organization to the NASD. For the purposes of this book we will be referring to the organization as FINRA/NASD. Sections of the FINRA codes and bylaws are copyrighted 2009 FINRA. All rights reserved. FINRA is the trademark of the Financial Industry Regulatory Authority, Inc. Reprinted with permission from FINRA.

Agency Principles

An agency relationship between an insurance professional and an insurance carrier gives the agent the power to sell insurance on behalf of carriers through their agency agreements. Through the agency agreement, the insurance professional is given the power to contractually bind the carrier. The power is fairly broad and has been used by the courts to extend the express authority granted an insurance agent by a carrier.

Agents also derive their authority from the agency contract. Typically, the agency contract specifically authorizes the agent to solicit insurance applications, describe coverage, and provide service to the company's policyowners. The agency contract may also authorize the insurance agent to collect premiums.

The power and authority granted by the agency agreement should not be confused with obtaining a state license. For example, an agent may be licensed to sell both life and health insurance in a particular state. The carrier, however, may only be involved in the life side of the insurance business. Under the agency agreement, the agent would only have the power and authority to solicit life insurance, not health insurance, for this particular carrier.

Types of Agent Authority

An agency relationship that binds the carrier can be created in several ways including:

- express authority
- implied authority
- apparent authority
- ratification

Express Authority

This type of authority is specifically spelled out and granted to the agent in the agency contract. An example of expressed authority is the authority of the insurance professional to solicit applications for the type of insurance sold by the carrier. For example, if Tom Black sold life insurance for ABC Company, Tom would have the authority, as an agent of ABC Company, to encourage potential customers to apply for ABC's products.

Few legal questions arise in regard to expressed authority, since the extent of this can be identified clearly from the terms of the agency contract, signed by the agent and the carrier.

Implied Authority

An agent has actual authority to act on the principal's behalf when he or she reasonably believes that such authority has been given. This type of authority is necessary, since the express authority given to an agent will not always articulate each aspect of the authority given to that agent. Implied authority was developed to cover the inevitable gaps which are found in every contract, no matter how carefully it is drawn up.

Usually, the agent is given implied authority to act in accordance with the general customs of business. It is implied that the agent can use all reasonable means to carry out the purpose of the agency agreement. For example, as a part of their express authority to solicit business, agents have the implied authority to explain the terms and conditions of particular financial products to potential clients.

Apparent Authority

This is the type of authority that gets insurance agents and their companies into the most legal trouble. In general, Party A is not legally responsible for the acts of Party B, simply because B says he was acting on A's behalf. However, A will be responsible if A has created the reasonable appearance of authority in B.

For example, Agent Burke has worked for AAA Life Insurance Company for several months. Due to poor production, Agent Burke's contract is terminated. However, Agent Burke retains her sales materials and other materials that identify her as a representative of AAA. Using these materials, she sells several products to Client Charles. Charles relies on the apparent authority Agent Burke seems to have by her use of the AAA materials, business cards, and stationary in her presentation.

Situations of apparent authority can also involve agents who are under contract but go beyond the terms of the agency agreement. For example, an agent may make credible statements regarding the terms of a financial product. Because the agent represents the company in the eyes of the client, the company can be bound for benefits beyond the terms of the contract.

Credibility
The word credible is the key to whether or not the notion of apparent authority will bind an insurer. If a statement is credible, it will generally be binding. If a statement is obviously outlandish, it will not.

Ratification

If an insurance professional sells a product that he or she is not licensed to sell, the company is not obligated to honor the insurance professional's acts. However, if the company issues the policy, it validates or ratifies the agent's act. Ratification, in other words, is the validation of an unauthorized act by the person or entity on whose behalf the action purportedly took place.

Implications of Agency

The agency contract between an agent and an insurer carries with it the following primary legal implications:

- The agent represents the interests of the carrier. This means the agent has legal responsibilities and obligations to the company as well as to the client.
- The agent is given power to act on behalf of the company. This power includes the power to enter into legal contracts on behalf of the insurer. For example, the agent can bind the carrier. In other words, the agent can create legal liability for the carrier under the insurance contract. The agent can also create legal rights for the carrier under the insurance contract.
- The acts of the agent are considered acts of the company.
- Knowledge of the agent is considered to be knowledge of the company. For example, if the agent has knowledge of health matters pertinent to the issuance of insurance, it is assumed that this information is also available to the carrier.

AGENT OBLIGATIONS TO PRODUCT CARRIER

Obligation of Loyalty

Agents owe a duty of loyalty to their companies. Agents must display the utmost good faith and integrity in dealing with their companies and must be scrupulously honest in handling all affairs dealing with respect to their carriers. Insofar as it is possible, agents should look out for the benefit of the company in all matters connected with their agency agreements.

Depending on their relationship with their carriers, financial services professionals have three potential roles under the law of agency:

- Captive agents solicit business on behalf of companies (or carriers).
- Brokers act on behalf of individual clients in order to secure products.
- Consultants provide advice regarding the type of products a consumer should purchase.

Obligation to Avoid Conflicts of Interest

Closely related to an agent's obligation of loyalty is his or her obligation to avoid conflicts of interest. This has slightly different meanings, depending upon whether or not the agent is a captive agent or an independent agent.

Generally speaking, captive agents are held to a stricter standard in this regard. For example, captive agents cannot serve two carriers that sell competing products at the same time. It may be possible, however, for captive agents to sell products not offered by their own carriers but sold through other carriers.

The wise course of action in this situation is for a captive agent to inform his or her carrier of the complete facts. In this way, the agent's carrier can determine whether or not there is a conflict of interest. This procedure also indicates the agent's adherence to strict ethical standards and serves to enhance and protect his or her reputation, preventing any inadvertent misunderstandings in the process.

Independent agents represent both carriers and clients at different points in the transaction. The client is represented during the selection process. Once a determination has been made in regard to the coverage to be selected, loyalty is owed to the carrier during the application, underwriting and record-keeping process.

Agents have an obligation to follow the lawful and reasonable instructions of their principals. This obligation is of particular importance in today's litigious environment. Many companies and product carriers provide strict instructions about the solicitation of business and client communication. This caution is understandable in light of a company's potential legal liability for the statements and communications of its agents.

Obligation of Careful Solicitation

Agents' jobs involve seeking out profitable business for their companies or carriers. This involves the careful selection of those prospects for whom the particular product would be suitable and who would be suitable for the product. For example, if the product is a life insurance product, then careful solicitation involves the selection of prospects who need it and can reasonably pay their initial and future premiums. For example, one should not target elderly people for deferred annuities with large surrender charges.

Obligation to Perform with Skill and Care

An agent has the obligation to make full disclosure of all pertinent information to the company or carrier. The point is that the principle has entrusted the agent to act on his or her behalf. The agent is required to disclose any and all information that could materially affect the interaction between the client and the company or product carrier, whether this information concerns the health, financial status or any other special circumstance of the client. Just as the client has a right to all relevant and material information about a particular financial product before making an informed decision to buy, the company or product carrier has a right to sufficient information to be able to make an informed decision about to whom it is in its interest to sell a particular product.

THE EMERGENCE OF FINANCIAL PLANNING SERVICES

Until the early 1980s, personal financial planning services were primarily available only to the wealthy. Such services were provided by the so-called "old line" investment advisors at a significant cost. However, with the advent of relative prosperity, middle-income Americans became more financially astute. But while gross personal incomes rose, mounting inflation and taxes absorbed greater portions of that income. To meet their retirement and other future financial needs, many individuals increasingly relied upon their own personal financial plans, either as a supplement to employer and/or government programs or, in some situations, as the primary foundation for their financial future. In doing so, however, many found that prudent selection from among a variety of investment and insurance alternatives had become an increasingly complex task. Thus, a substantial demand for relatively low-cost financial planning services emerged.

Who is considered a financial planner? In the context of life insurance, an agent who sells only insurance products and provides little or no other financial services would not be deemed a financial planner. However, when an agent moves beyond simply advising upon and selling life insurance and offers financial advice in general, he or she has moved into the realm of financial planning.

Sensing an opportunity, like other financial institutions, many life insurers began to position themselves within the newly emerging financial services marketplace not only to offer an array of diverse financial products (especially investment-oriented products), but also to expand the scope of their activities to provide financial planning services.

Furthermore, by the 1980s, the competitive trend toward products with lower premiums, including less expensive term insurance, portended lower commissions for insurance agents, per unit of sale. Life insurance agents felt threatened not only by this trend, but also by inflationary and other cost pressures of doing business. Consequently, life agents (as well as their companies) sought additional strategies for increasing income. Within this environment, many agents responded affirmatively to the opportunity to offer more comprehensive financial services, including not only more diverse insurance and/or other products, such as mutual funds, but also a broader scope of financial planning services.

A financial planner has been described as a person who offers individualized advice on investments, life insurance and the overall general management of financial affairs with a view toward planning, implementing and maintaining a program designed to meet the client's future financial needs.

Financial planning typically involves providing a variety of services, principally advisory in nature, to individuals or families regarding the management of their financial resources based upon an analysis of individual clients' needs. Generally, financial planning services involve preparing a financial program for a client, based on the client's financial circumstances and objectives. This information normally would cover present and anticipated assets and liabilities, including insurance, savings, investments and anticipated retirement or other employee benefits. The program developed for the client usually includes general recommendations for a course of activity or specific actions to be taken by the client. For example, recommendations may be made that the client obtain insurance or revise existing coverage, establish an individual retirement account, increase or decrease funds held in savings accounts or invest funds in securities. A financial planner may develop tax or estate plans for clients, or refer clients to an accountant or attorney for these services.

In most cases, the provider of such financial planning services assists the client in implementing the recommended program by, among other things, making specific recommendations to carry out the general recommendation of the program, or by selling the client insurance products, securities or other investments. The financial planner may also review the client's program periodically and recommend revisions. Persons providing such financial planning services use various compensation arrangements.[25]

There are three types of personal individual financial planners. First, there is the "fee-only" type, who charges his or her clients a fee for the development of a financial plan but does not recommend specific investments, insurance contracts and/or other type of products. Second, there is the "commission-only" type of planner, who charges no fees for the development of a financial plan, but collects a commission on the securities, insurance or other products or services that he or she sells to the client. Third, there is the "fee-commission" type, who charges the client a fee for the planning services rendered and receives commissions for the sale of products. Regardless of the approach adopted, the offering of financial planning services was, and still is, seen as a means to increase one's wealth and/or income.

Furthermore, the emergence of financial planning services on a broader basis to the less affluent population has not been confined to life insurers and their agents. As the demand for financial planning increased, accountants, lawyers, banks and securities firms have become increasingly involved. Boundaries of traditional disciplines were breached as these persons and institutions advertised themselves as full financial planners.

Within this environment, both actual and potential abuses have occurred. Many of the so-called financial planners lacked even the most basic qualifications to competently perform financial planning tasks. Often, they used their financial planning status to sell securities of issuers or insurance of insurers with which they were affiliated. Because of the rapid growth in the number of persons and firms offering financial planning services and the accompanying abuses associated with such growth, there has been increased focus upon the applicability of both federal and state regulatory law to the financial planning phenomenon. The activities of financial planners,

---

25. SEC Rel. No. IA-1092, October 8, 1987.

both individuals and organizations, cut across various regulatory disciplines at both the federal and state levels, giving rise to a complex system of dual federal and multistate regulation.

FEDERAL REGULATION OF REGISTERED PRODUCTS

Historical Background

It has been many years since the 1929 stock market crash, but the regulatory responses to this crisis remain with us. Federal investigations at the time of the 1929 crash recognized that market manipulation, overextension of credit for stock purchases and unfair dealings with clients were abuses in need of correction.

In response, Congress enacted several major laws that changed the structure of the securities market in the United States. The acts provided a definition of securities, guidelines for the issuance and registration of security products and rules regarding the conduct of security marketplace operations. These acts also provided for the establishment of self-regulatory organizations, such as the National Association of Securities Dealers (NASD). In July 2007, the NASD merged with the member regulation, enforcement and arbitration functions of the New York Stock Exchange and is now called the Financial Industry Regulatory Authority (FINRA). FINRA oversees over 5,000 brokerage firms, about 172,000 branch offices, and more than 676,000 registered securities representatives.

A general familiarity with three federal acts is helpful to understand what is appropriate conduct for businesses in today's financial services marketplace. These acts are the Securities Act of 1933, the Securities Exchange Act of 1934, and the Investment Advisers Act of 1940. All share a common statutory theme—providing proper disclosure, which is necessary to a free and open marketplace. From an ethical standpoint, the acts share a common focus of fair and honest dealings in the securities marketplace.

Securities Act of 1933

The Securities Act of 1933 provides statutory guidelines that must be followed before a company can sell new issues of its stock to the public. These guidelines emphasize disclosure of information. This disclosure is accomplished through the completion of a registration statement, which must be reviewed by the Securities and Exchange Commission (SEC). Following the filing of the registration statement, a prospectus is prepared. The prospectus summarizes the information contained in the registration statement and must be made available to all interested buyers.

Securities Exchange Act of 1934

While the Securities Act of 1933 concerns newly issued securities, the Securities Exchange Act of 1934 extends federal regulation to the ongoing trading of securities that have already been issued. The 1934 Act charged the SEC with the enforcement of these directives.

Provisions of the 1934 Act require disclosure of information by publicly traded companies, prohibit market manipulation, and restrict the amount of credit that may be extended for the purchase of securities. The 1934 Act also requires security brokers and dealers to register with the SEC. In addition, the 1934 Act provides for SEC supervision of national security exchanges, industry associations, and securities information processors.

The primary function of the SEC is to review information provided in the registration statement and other forms submitted to its offices. The SEC does not provide the public with investment advice. It is up to individual investors and/or their advisors to evaluate the securities registered with the SEC.

Investment Advisers Act of 1940

The Investment Advisers Act of 1940 seeks to protect the public from harmful and fraudulent conduct of persons who are compensated to advise others on buying and/or selling securities. It was aimed at two categories of advisors: those who publish market reports or newsletters for paying subscribers which contain recommendations concerning securities, and those who advise individual clients about securities. A major purpose of the law is to reveal conflicts of interests that may cause the advisor to make recommendations more in the advisor's own interest than in the client's interest.

This act sets out federal regulations for investment advisors. The key question for financial services professionals posed by the Act is whether or not they are considered investment advisors. If they are, they are required to register with the SEC. For the purposes of the Investment Advisers Act of 1940, an investment advisor is defined as any person who, for compensation, is engaged in the business of either (a) providing advice to others or (b) issuing reports and analysis regarding securities.

There are some instances where it is unclear whether or not an agent is an investment advisor. For example, if an agent advertises a financial planning designation, is he or she providing financial advice in the ordinary course of business? In a few cases, state law points to a "yes" answer. In other cases, the answer is unclear; in still others, the answer is "no." Failure to comply with the law's provisions carries heavy penalties, so many legal commentators suggest that agents should register, if in doubt.

One other thought to keep in mind: registration under the Investment Advisers Act is just registration. It is not an endorsement of competence or expertise by the SEC. This means financial services professionals should avoid the temptation to imply that. We will look at the Investment Advisers Act later in this chapter.

REGULATION OF BROKER DEALERS AND THE FINANCIAL INDUSTRY REGULATORY AUTHORITY (FINRA)

The SEC is not the sole source of rules and regulations under the federal securities laws. In drafting the Depression Era legislation, Congress recognized that the nation's stock exchanges had long been regulating the trading activities of their own members. With this in mind, self-regulatory organizations (SROs) were incorporated into the regulatory structure of the securities industry.

The National Association of Securities Dealers was a part of this self-regulatory structure. It was established under authority granted by 1938 amendments to the Securities Exchange Act of 1934. The principle behind the enabling legislation is voluntary self-regulation of broker/dealers under SEC oversight. As noted earlier, in July 2007, the NASD joined forces with the New York Stock Exchange Regulation, a wholly owned subsidiary of the New York Stock Exchange LLC to form FINRA. According to the SEC, whose approval was required to complete the merger, "The consolidation is intended to help streamline the broker-dealer regulatory system, combine technologies, and permit the establishment of a single set of rules governing membership matters, with the aim of enhancing oversight of U.S. securities firms and assuring investor protection."

FINRA has the power to require and monitor compliance with standardized rules of fair practice for the industry. FINRA regulatory responsibilities include registration and testing of securities professionals, review of members' advertising and sales literature and services such as arbitration of investor disputes. Registered representatives must provide FINRA with personal information, including prior employment and any history of securities-related disciplinary action. The Securities and Exchange Act of 1934 regulates brokers and dealers. For the purposes of this chapter, we will use the definitions provided in each of these acts and used by the SEC. A broker is defined as an individual who conducts transactions in securities on the behalf of others. A dealer is defined as an individual who buys securities for his or her own account.

While these terms may appear to be clear cut, trends in the 1990s blurred any bright lines between individuals who identify themselves as broker dealers and those who identify themselves as investment advisors.

Most broker-dealers need to be registered with the SEC. The only exception is if they deal only with government and municipal securities or do business entirely within one state. In addition, each individual broker-dealer must be a member of FINRA.

FINRA

As mentioned above, the SEC granted the NASD, and now FINRA, the responsibility for regulating this aspect of the financial services industry. In order do so appropriately, FINRA developed a series of "regulatory conduct" rules which will be reviewed below.

- *Suitability:* According to NASD Rule 2310, "In recommending to a customer the purchase, sale or exchange of any security, a member shall have reasonable grounds for believing that the recommendation is suitable for such customer upon the basis of the facts, if any, disclosed by such customer as to his other security holdings and as to his financial situation and needs." Specifically, in order to sell a suitable product, it is necessary to discover four things: (1) the customer's financial status; (2) his or her tax status; (3) his or her investment objectives and (4) other information used or considered reasonable by such member or registered representative in making recommendations.

  The issue of suitability has been a topic of heated discussions in recent years. An area of particular interest to both regulators and industry practitioners concerns the question of whether certain products are unsuitable for entire classes of investors, such as

Equity Indexed Annuities (EIA) for seniors. Many states have passed legislation that mandates additional protection for seniors regarding the sale of EIAs.

- *Prohibition of Excessive Mark-Ups:* In Rule IM 2440-1, which deals with "mark ups," FINRA states the following: "It shall be deemed a violation . . . for a member to enter into any transaction with a customer in any security at any price not reasonably related to the current market price of the security or to charge a commission which is not reasonable." FINRA continues to support a 5 percent mark-up as a general guideline, which has been the standard since 1943, although this is certainly not a rule. The determination of prices can depend on any of the following factors: the type of security involved; the availability of the security in the marketplace; the price of the security; the amount of money in the transactions; disclosure; the pattern of a member's mark ups; and the nature of the member's business.

- *Prohibition of Excessive Trading:* In Rule IM 2310-2, FINRA specifically prohibits churning. Churning is defined as excessive trading in a client's account in order to maximize commissions, without taking into account the best interest of the client. There are three characteristics of churning: (1) the broker-dealer has discretionary control over the account; (2) while there are not specific standards to measure excessive trading, there is a cause for concern when the account is turned over more than four times its total value annually and (3) the intent of the trading is to generate commissions. The prohibition against churning represents a part of a larger injunction to FINRA members to treat their clients fairly. The sales dealings should be judged against this standard of fairness, rather than profit.

- *Supervision Requirements*: Rule 3010 requires that each FINRA member who employs broker dealers appropriately supervise all registered representatives to ensure that they are in compliance with their regulatory and legal obligations. This supervision includes, but is not limited to, requiring that each member investigate the good character, business repute, qualifications, and experience" of a job applicant before the member applies to register that applicant with FINRA.

- *Best Execution*: Rule 2320 states that the FINRA member is required to act with "reasonable diligence" to ensure that the customer received the most favorable terms under prevailing marketing conditions

- *Record Keeping*: Rule 3010 states that broker-dealers are required to keep a number of records regarding their businesses. The type and format of this record keeping is specified in the SEC Rule 17 a-3 and 17 a-4 of the Securities and Exchange Act of 1934.

Broker-Dealers and the Question of Fiduciary Duties

Whether broker-dealers should be considered fiduciaries is a question that recently sparked a great deal of debate among corporations, practitioners and regulatory organizations. While it is clear that Registered Investment Advisors (RIAs) are held to the standard of a fiduciary, whether the relationships that broker-dealers have with their clients rises to that level is a different question.

Whether the broker has discretionary authority over the account of his or her client is of great importance in determining whether the broker is involved in a fiduciary relationship. A discretionary account is one in which the client has given permission for the broker to purchase and sell securities on his or her behalf without expressed consent for each transaction, but often within preexisting parameters. When a broker-dealer has discretionary authority, he or she is given the permission to substitute his or her own judgment for the judgment of the client. Insofar as the broker-dealer is acting as a representative of the client, without explicit oversight, he or she is required to act in the best interest of the client. In *Leib v. Merrill Lynch, Pierce, Fenner and Smith, Inc.* the court ruled that brokers handling discretionary accounts owe a broad spectrum of fiduciary duties to their clients. Brokers who do not have discretionary authority over the funds of their clients do not, for the most part, owe them a fiduciary duty. However, the same court case, stated that brokers assisting with nondiscretionary accounts have a limited set of duties.

If the main factor of whether a client is owed fiduciary concern by his or her broker is whether or not the broker has discretionary control over the client's account, it is important to know whether a broker has this level of control or access. Unfortunately, whether an account is discretionary or nondiscretionary is not always clear. A broker who is handling a nondiscretionary account for client could begin to exercise control over the account, with or without the client's consent. The court has found that, even when the brokers kept their clients continuously appraised of their actions, the fact that the brokers acted as through they had discretionary authority created a fiduciary obligation where one did not previously exist.

THE INVESTMENT ADVISERS ACT?

The SEC takes the position that the Investment Advisers Act of 1940 governs the behavior of financial planners. The Act defines an investment advisor as any person who, for compensation, engages in the business of advising others as to the value of securities or the advisability of acquiring or disposing of securities. Any person who falls within the Advisers Act definition of an investment advisor (unless expressly excluded from the definition or exempted from the registration requirements) and who makes use of the mails or any instrumentality of interstate commerce is required to register with the SEC pursuant to the Act.

In 1987, the SEC issued the Investment Advisers Act Release No. 1092, which defined three elements that must be met if persons or entities to qualify as investment advisors under the Act. The SEC, in order to protect clients from fraudulent and abusive situations, issued three tests that could be used to determine whether or not an individual must register as an investment advisor. If all three tests are answered in the affirmative, registration is required. If any of the tests are answered in the negative, there is no need for the individual to become a Registered Investment Advisor (RIA).

1. They must give advice or analysis concerning securities.
2. They must be engaged in the business of advising others regarding securities.
3. They must be in receipt of compensation for such advise.

What is a security. The Supreme Court defined what constitutes a security in the 1946 landmark case *SEC v. T.W. Howey Co.* The Court ruled that

> "The test is whether the scheme involves an investment of money in a common enterprise with profits to come solely from the efforts of others."

Under this test, virtually every investment which a financial planner might recommend for his or her client would appear to qualify as a security. Hence, the term *security* has been interpreted to include not only marketable securities traded on an organized exchange (such as the New York Stock Exchange), but also such instruments as limited partnerships, mutual funds, certificates of deposit, commercial paper, variable annuities and variable life insurance, as well as other types of interest-sensitive life insurance products. However, merely dealing with a security does not, by itself, make someone an investment advisor. The SEC has two tests to determine whether someone is an investment advisor.

Security Advice Test

If an individual provides advice or issues reports or analyses regarding specific securities, clearly this individual is an investment adviser. this test is met. However, the advice need not relate to specific securities, but may focus on the advisability of investing in securities in general. The SEC has determined that a person who deals with securities in general, or who advises as to the advantages and disadvantages of investing in securities vis-à-vis other financial vehicles (for example, life insurance), meets this test. Additionally, most analyses or reports that incorporate judgments concerning securities are considered to be investment advice. Given the breadth of the definition of a security, virtually any person who presents himself or herself as a financial planning professional almost assuredly will render advice concerning securities.

Security Business Test

Providing advice with some regularity, even when it is not the person's primary business activity, is an important factor in subjecting the person to the requirements of the act. Whether a person is "in the business" is determined by a facts and circumstances analysis, including consideration of the frequency of the activity. Furthermore, a person is deemed to be "in the business" if he or she does any of the following:

- holds himself or herself out as an investment advisor
- receives separate or additional compensation that is a clearly definable charge for providing advice about securities
- provides specific investment advice in other than isolated instances

Another way of looking at this is to examine how the individual presents his or her business to the public. For example, what name and type of business description appears in the telephone book or on the front door? Does the individual's business card or letterhead suggest he or she is an investment advisor or stockbroker? If the way an individual presents his or her business to the public suggests that investment advice is provided, the second test provides another factor indicating the need for the individual to be a Registered Investment Advisor (RIA).

REGULATION UNDER THE INVESTMENT ADVISERS ACT

The basic regulatory mechanism of the Advisers Act is the requirement that any person falling within the definition of an investment advisor, unless excluded or exempted by another section of the statute, must register with the SEC. A financial planner, as an investment advisor (which is usually the case, unless for some reason, the person is exempted or excluded), is subject to a number of legal obligations in addition to the registration requirement.

- First, under its broad rule-making authority, the SEC has imposed extensive record-keeping and reporting requirements. The SEC generally requires that an investment advisor maintain typical accounting books and records (such as checkbooks, banking statements, and written agreements), as well as certain additional records (including personal securities transactions entered into by the advisor and his or her employee) to ensure compliance with fiduciary standards.

- Second, an investment advisor is subject to inspection and examination by the SEC. Inspections are of two types—routine and "for cause." Inspectors especially look for evidence of churning, scalping, practices contrary to the client's interest, unsuitability, deceptive advertising and improper record-keeping.

- Third, while almost any basis of compensation may be used (as long as it is not fraudulent), an investment advisor is prohibited from entering into an investment advisory contract if the contract provides for compensation based upon a share of the capital gains or capital appreciation of the client's funds. Underlying this prohibition is the concern that the investment advisor might undertake undue investment risks with the client's funds in efforts to enhance the advisor's compensation.

- Fourth, every investment advisor, when entering into an advisory contract, must deliver a written disclosure statement (often referred to as the "brochure") to the prospective client at least 2 days before the advisory contract is entered into or at the time of entering into the contract if the client can terminate the contract within 5 days. This statement must include information concerning the advisor's background, education, experience, types of services offered and the investment techniques to be employed.

- Fifth, the Act prohibits an investment advisor from representing that he or she is an "investment counsel," unless his or her principal business consists of action as an investment advisor and a substantial portion of the business consists of providing investment advisory services.

- Sixth, an investment advisor is permitted to pay finder's fees, but only if certain conditions are met. There must be a written agreement between the advisor and the finder of the business. The finder must provide the prospective client not only with a copy of the advisor's brochure, but also a separate disclosure statement that outlines the arrangement between the advisor and the finder, including the compensation to be paid by the advisor to the finder and whether the client will be charged for this service in addition to the advisory fee. The SEC does not look favorably on this method of obtaining new business, so if this method is used, great care should be taken to comply with all requirements.

- Seventh, during the legislative process leading up to the enactment of the Adviser Act, much emphasis was placed on the importance of trust and confidence between an investment advisor and his or her clients. As a consequence, the Act contains an antifraud section detailing various types of conduct considered to be violative of the fiduciary nature of the investment advisory relationship. Among other things, the Act specifically prohibits the use of the mails or any means of interstate commerce to "employ any device, scheme, or artifice to defraud a client or prospective client" or "to engage in any transaction, practice or course of business which operates as a fraud or deceit upon any client or prospective client." The United States Supreme Court elaborated on the obligations by defining an investment advisor as a fiduciary owing his or her clients an affirmative duty of utmost good faith and full and fair disclosure of all material facts, as well as an affirmative obligation to employ reasonable care to avoid misleading his or her clients.

The SEC has stated that the duty of an investment advisor to refrain from fraudulent activity includes the affirmative obligations to:

- disclose all material facts as to any potential conflicts of interest so the client can make an informed judgment whether to enter into or to continue the relationship with the investment advisor

- disclose fully the nature and extent of any interest the advisor has in any given recommendation

- inform clients of their right to execute recommended investment purchases or sales through other broker-dealers

- disclose whether the advisor's personal securities transactions are inconsistent with advice rendered to a client

- avoid engaging in any conduct that might result in the advisor preferring his or her own interests to those of clients

The antifraud provisions of the Advisors Act apply to any person who is an investment advisor as defined by the Act, whether or not such a person is required to be registered with the SEC as an investment advisor. Although persons who are excluded from the definition of an investment advisor are not subject to the antifraud provisions, those who fall within the definition of an investment advisor, even though not required to be registered, are subject to the antifraud provisions of the Advisors Act and the rules promulgated thereunder.

REQUIREMENTS OF A REGISTERED INVESTMENT ADVISOR

- *Registration:* The first step in becoming an RIA is to register with the SEC. Registration involves the completion of a detailed questionnaire (Form ADV) and the submission of a onetime filing fee.

- *Records:* RIAs are required to keep extensive records regarding the many aspects of their practices. This record keeping involves retention of sales brochures, client communications and recommendations. It also involves maintenance of financial records, in accordance with generally accepted accounting principles.

- *Fee Restrictions:* RIAs are subject to the fee restrictions developed under SEC rules. As a general rule of thumb, the fee restrictions tend to be stricter for clients with assets of less than one million dollars.

- *Designation Prohibition:* The term "RIA" cannot be used as a designation as one would use LUTCF, CLU, or ChFC because it merely represents a registration, not an educational achievement. However, the rules do permit those registered to spell out fully and refer to their status as registered investment advisor(s) when dealing with clients.

- *Informational Brochure:* RIAs must develop and distribute a brochure to clients, which includes substantial information about their education, business background and clientele. The brochure must also indicate the type of informational sources used and the investment strategies pursued.

- *Client Reassignment:* RIAs cannot arbitrarily reassign their clients to other RIA's. Clients must clearly consent to any reassignment. This rule stresses the personal nature of the relationship and the uniqueness of services provided by RIAs. (This is also a factor that RIAs must keep in mind when planning for their retirement. Simply put, RIAs cannot decide to sell their practices without notifying clients. Preretirement succession planning thus becomes an important element for any RIA. In this way, clients can get to know the "newcomer" during a transition period and can then make informed decisions as to how they wish their accounts to be handled.)
- *Fiduciary Role:* The Investment Advisers Act of 1940 contains strict antifraud provisions. These provisions have the effect of recognizing RIAs as fiduciaries who owe their clients affirmative duties. These duties include the obligation to deal in good faith and to provide full and fair disclosure of all material facts that surround an investment recommendation. As fiduciaries, RIAs must also be careful not to place themselves in ethically questionable situations that involve conflicts of interests.

THE MERRILL RULE CHANGES THE GAME

Under the 1940 Investment Adviser Act, registered brokers and dealers are excluded from the terms of the Act if:

1. Any advice that the broker-dealer gives to clients is "solely incidental" to its business as a broker dealer.
2. The broker-dealer does not receive any "special compensation" for rendering such advice.

It was unclear how the SEC understood "solely incidental" and "special compensation." When does the "advice-giving" aspect of one's business become more than incidental? The SEC offered various attempts to clarify its meaning, stating that advice was more than "solely incidental" when the broker either had discretionary authority over the client's account or when he or she was focusing comments on a client's entire portfolio rather than on one particular product. Another distinction was made between a financial plan and financial planning services. A financial plan is a more comprehensive proposal that can include recommendations about insurance, savings, tax and estate planning and investments. On the other hand, financial planning services focus on explicating how a particular product or service fits into the client's long-term strategy. The former would be considered more than incidental advice, while the latter would be covered by the exclusion.

The prohibition against receiving "special compensation" was also unclear. The real distinction seemed to be the difference between a broker-dealer who charges transaction-specific fees and investment advisors who charge one general fee.

In 1999, the SEC attempted to clarify the boundary between broker-dealers and investment advisors through a Notice of Proposed Rule Making. Rule 202, often referred to as the "Merrill Rule," stated that broker-dealers could be exempted from the 1940 Investment Adviser Act while offering fee-based accounts if they did the following:

1. The broker dealer did not exercise investment discretion over the brokerage accounts.
2. Any advice provided by the broker-dealers with respect to the accounts was incidental to the brokerage services provided to these accounts.
3. Prominent disclosure was made to the client regarding the fact that the amount was a brokerage account and not an advisory account.

In April 2005, the SEC finalized the Rule in "Certain Broker-Dealers Deemed Not To Be Investment Advisers." The Rule was revised from the 1999 version by expanded disclosure-statement requirements, additional clarification regarding the definition of "solely incidental advice," and the understanding that broker-dealers must register as investment advisors if they charge a separate fee or offer separate contracts for advisory services and if they hold themselves out as financial planners. However, Rule 202 raised the ire of industry groups and, in particular, the Financial Planners Association (FPA), which believed that the SEC had overstepped its regulatory authority by nullifying aspects of the 1940 Investment Advisors Act. In addition, the FPA contended that Rule 202 would blur the distinction between investments advisors and broker-dealers in the minds of members of the investing public. A distinction could have dire consequences since, as we have stated, broker-dealers are held to a lower standard of concern and care for the best interests of their clients.

In March of 2007, the U.S. Court of Appeals for the District of Columbia agreed with the FPA and invalidated Rule 202. The basis for the court's decision was that the SEC was overreaching its authority as an administrative agency. In May 2007, in a move that surprised many industry watchers, the SEC announced that it would not appeal the decision.

The SEC's attempt to illuminate the boundary between broker-dealers and investment advisors was ultimately unsuccessful. However, it is still unclear at what point brokers are acting in such a way as to necessitate registering as investment advisors, both for their own protection and the protection of their clients. Obviously, this is a key issue that will continue to unfold in the future, and one that deserves careful attention.

CASE STUDY: INVESTMENT ADVICE—FINRA RULES

Marvin Atwood has been an insurance agent for the past 7 years. From the start, he has been licensed to sell traditional life, health and annuity products. Last month, Marvin obtained a Series 6 license. This permits him to sell his company's recently introduced variable life insurance product portfolio.

During the past year he has also completed financial planning courses that permit him to use a designation. He is currently debating whether to change his business card to read, Marvin Atwood, Atwood Certified Financial and Investment Planning."

For the past year, he has been following the movement of the stock market. Day after day, he has read about the growing shift of household wealth into financial assets. Marvin now feels he can put this knowledge to work. He believes that the new variable product line will open many new sales opportunities. In fact, he has scheduled an appointment with a new client, Loretta Charles, and intends to make his first variable life sale.

During his meeting with Loretta, Marvin used a company-provided fact finder. At the initial interview, Marvin learned that Loretta recently inherited a half interest in a condominium from her father. The property is under contract, and Loretta expects to net $30,000 from its sale. Loretta has followed the stock market headlines, but has traditionally placed her savings in certificates of deposit and money market funds.

Marvin also learned that Loretta is a middle-aged, single mother. She bears the full financial responsibility for raising her 16-year-old son, Jeffrey. During their meeting, Loretta expressed two concerns in regard to her parental financial responsibilities. Number one, she is concerned about having funds available to meet Jeffrey's needs should she die prematurely. Number two, she is concerned about meeting college tuition bills.

That evening, Marvin went through the investment books and magazines he had gathered during the last year. He clipped a few articles on the growth opportunities offered by the stock market. He even found an article that mentioned a mutual fund (ABCO Growth) sold through his company. Marvin put these together with a personal note directing Loretta to read the materials. He felt these to be superior to the dry materials drafted by his home office.

The following week Marvin met with Loretta again. He started the meeting by providing her with an embossed folder—"Financial and Investment Plan for Loretta Charles." Marvin then proceeded to review his recommendations. He first recommended that Loretta provide for her life insurance needs through the purchase of a variable universal life policy. He then recommended that Loretta place at least half of her expected inheritance in the ABCO Growth Fund. Marvin based his recommendations on the long-term upward trend of the stock market, as cited in the previously-sent articles.

Loretta thanked Marvin for his work and indicated that she would need at least a week to think over his recommendations. Marvin ended this meeting by reminding Loretta that a delay could mean a major market movement and a missed opportunity to time the market.

Key Points to Ponder
1. Is Marvin selling on the basis of needs analysis or preconceived needs? If he is selling on the basis of preconceived needs, does this technique raise ethical issues?
2. Is it advisable to use company-approved materials in selling to clients?
3. Are there any compliance rules that must be followed when selling equity-type products?
4. Has Marvin taken into consideration the dictates of the FINRA Rules of Conduct in his dealings with Loretta? Explain.
5. Is Marvin properly representing his professional role in this sales situation? Explain.

SUMMARY

This chapter has looked at the relationship of ethics and the law. While the law is the public's agency for enforcing moralities, acting legally is not always acting ethically. So, we study law because it is a prime step leading us in the direction of ethical behavior, and what is legal is usually ethical. However, financial services professionals are subject to both federal and state laws. Laws at both levels impact the products and selling practices of financial services professionals.

Financial services professionals act as agents. Agency is based on the principles of power and authority. Authority may be expressed, implied, or apparent. Unauthorized acts of an insurance agent may be ratified later by a carrier.

Financial services professionals owe fiduciary obligations to their carriers and clients. The extent of these fiduciary obligations depends on whether the professional is acting as an agent or broker. Agent fiduciary obligations include loyalty, careful solicitation and full disclosure.

Brokers owe their prime fiduciary loyalty to their clients in placing insurance. Brokers do, however, have fiduciary responsibilities toward carriers, such as the remission of premium payments. Insurance agents operating as consultants or financial planners owe broad fiduciary responsibilities to their clients. All financial services professionals should pay particular attention to the mandates of state law and licensing requirements.

To ensure as much freedom to its citizens as possible, governments establish laws as a minimum standard, or as Paine phrased it, "moral mediocrity." Many aspire to much higher standards. We could depend on the ethical or moral standards of our society, but there may be disagreement about some of those and how they apply to the specific subcultures to which we belong. Hence, to promulgate desirable modes of behavior, professions and industries have traditionally supplied their practitioners with codes of ethics. For example, the Hippocratic Oath that doctors still abide by goes back to the days of ancient Grecian society.

In conclusion, financial services professionals must take account of the limitations of laws and regulations. They are an important, but not the only, source of guidance. They do not take the place of personal reactions, professional codes, or the moral guidelines. Mere compliance with the law is not enough. One must act as a professional. What is involved in fulfilling the ethical obligations of a profession is covered in the next chapter.

CHAPTER REVIEW QUESTIONS

Answers to Review Questions are found in the Appendix.

1. Agency involves what two basic concepts?

    (A) law and ethics
    (B) liability and power
    (C) authority and liability
    (D) authority and power

2. The "Merrill Rule" would have exempted broker-dealers from the requirements of the 1940 Investment Advisers Act if they met all of the following conditions EXCEPT:

    (A) did not exercise investment discretion over the account
    (B) had been in the financial services profession for over 15 year
    (C) provided advice which was solely incidental to the management of the account
    (D) clearly disclosed to the client that the account was a brokerage account and not an advisory account

3. What characteristic makes the financial services professional more than a commodity salesperson?

    (A) the desire to bring a value-added service to others
    (B) an advanced degree from a prestigious university
    (C) multiple years of experience in the financial services industry
    (D) he sells products on commission

4. Which of the following types of relationships entails a high level of trust and the obligation to act according to high ethical standards of conduct?

    (A) professional relationship
    (B) fiduciary relationship
    (C) business relationship
    (D) working relationship

5. What type of financial services professional solicits business exclusively on behalf of an insurance carrier?

    (A) captive agent
    (B) broker
    (C) consultant
    (D) financial planner

6. What is the goal of compliance?

    (A) to hassle hard-working financial services professionals
    (B) to establish or reestablish ethical behavior
    (C) to create additional opportunities for underemployed
    (D) to detract from the client experience through mandating excessive paperwork

7. Which of the following types of agent authority involves the validation of an unauthorized act by the person or entity on whose behalf the action purportedly took place?

    (A) express authority
    (B) implied authority
    (C) apparent authority
    (D) ratification

8. In 2007, the NASD (National Association of Securities Dealers) and the NYSE (New York Stock Exchange) merged to form what organization?

    (A) Securities and Exchange Commission (SEC)
    (B) Public Companies Accounting Oversight Board (PCAOB)
    (C) Environmental Protection Agency (EPA)
    (D) Financial Industry Regulatory Authority (FINRA)

9. All of the following are general guidelines that should help agents avoid confusion about the nature of their fiduciary duties to their carriers, EXCEPT

    (A) Agents represent their insurer when insurance is being placed.
    (B) Agents represent their insurer in maintaining policyholder records.
    (C) Agents represent themselves when delivering insurance policies.
    (D) Agents represent their insurer when premiums are collected.

10. If compliance is defined as meeting the "letter of the law," how should we understand ethics?

    (A) as an unnecessary addition to compliance
    (B) as an obligation to perform with skill and care
    (C) as being identical in meaning with compliance
    (D) as an unrealistic demand upon harried and over-worked professionals

none of this wrong

Spirit of the law See page 4.4 & 4.5

Learning Objectives

An understanding of the material in this chapter should enable the student to

1. Identify the four characteristics of being a professional.

2. Describe the way the practice of financial services meets each of the seven basic requirements for being considered a profession.

3. List the ten expectations a client has of a professional.

4. List and describe the responsibilities of the financial services professional.

5. List seven practical steps that a financial services professional can use in order to avoid legal liability

6. Identify the seven common themes in the codes of ethics applicable to the financial services professional.

7. List five professional responsibility guidelines found in the financial services industry's professional codes.

THE FINANCIAL SERVICES PROFESSIONAL

We have seen that a primary ethical responsibility is to live up to one's commitments. Consequently, the decision to act as a professional imposes obligations on people. The fact that you are taking this course, or the fact that your company or employer requires you to get a professional designation and that you concur, means that you are making a commitment to act as a professional.

Years ago, there was an advertisement used by a financial consulting investment company. It presented a picture of a sales manager entreating his sales force "to unload this dog." In short, this was a picture of a manager encouraging his salespeople to sell an inferior product to whomever (client) they can persuade to buy it. The advertisement made it clear that a respectable company does not engage in this kind of behavior. The respectable company looks out for the interests of the client, handles reliable products and makes sure the products are suitable for the client. In short, the respectable company expects its sales force, distributors and agents to act as professionals.

The value of professionalism in the financial services industry has a long history. In 1915, in an address delivered before the annual meetings of Baltimore Life and New York Life Underwriters, Solomon S. Huebner, the founder of The American College, laid out his lifetime dream—to turn the life insurance salesperson into a professional. This dream motivated him, along with a group of insurance industry leaders, to establish The American College in 1927 as an institution which would educate insurance salespeople and award them a designation—the CLU (Chartered Life Underwriter)—which indicated they had achieved a certain level of expertise. The College required, and it still does today, that each designee pledge to serve the interests of the client. It was the dream of Dr. Huebner that each person graduating from The American College fulfill the characteristics of being a professional.

CHARACTERISTICS OF A PROFESSIONAL

Using physicians, lawyers, teachers and others as models of what professionals should be, Dr. Huebner crafted as fine a statement of what it takes to be a professional as any that exists; one that is as valid today as in 1915. He cited four characteristics of the professional.

1. The professional is involved in a vocation that is useful and noble enough to inspire love and enthusiasm in the practitioner.
2. The professional's vocation requires an expert's knowledge in its practice.
3. The professional should abandon the strictly selfish commercial view and ever keep in mind the advantage of the client."
4. The professional should possess a spirit of loyalty to fellow practitioners, of helpfulness to the common cause they all profess and should not allow any unprofessional acts to bring shame upon the entire profession.

It is evident that rendering financial services is a useful occupation, and the fact that financial planning helps people alleviate anxiety and gain security makes it a noble vocation. Thus, involvement in financial services meets Dr. Huebner's first characteristic of a professional.

The second characteristic is expert knowledge. Clearly, the practice of financial services is complicated and requires study to achieve competence and expertise. To stay abreast of the latest developments in financial instruments, and to know which products are beneficial to different clients, requires ongoing study.

The third characteristic that Dr. Huebner listed is the most interesting characteristic of the professional for our purposes because it lays out an ethical prescription. It requires the professional to "abandon the strictly selfish commercial view and ever keep in mind the advantage of the client."

The "strictly selfish commercial view" is the view that the principal concern of business is to make money or increase profit. It is the view of those whose only concern is to sell a product, without regard for the needs of the client. The "strictly selfish commercial point of view" distorts the position of Adam Smith, who is often considered the father of the capitalistic free-market economy. Smith, the 18th century economist-philosopher, in his book *The Wealth of Nations*, believed that a great deal of good comes from a system that allows people to pursue their own interests. Smith's view became the theoretical foundation and justification of the capitalist free-market economic system. However, according to Smith, the pursuit of self-interest must be constrained by ethical considerations of justice and fairness. Hence, one should not always look out for one's own interest. There are times when it is ethically necessary to constrain that self-interest in the name of justice or fairness.

It is perfectly acceptable to pursue our own interests. Smith's unique contribution was to understand how our natural self love and preferment will ultimately work for the betterment of society. In this way, it seems that if we don't have a healthy self-love and self-interest, we do both our neighbors and ourselves a disservice. Nevertheless, if we pursue our self-interest at the expense of another, we act unethically.

Because a "strictly selfish commercial view" encourages the pursuit of self-interest with no limits, it is a pursuit that inevitably leads to selfishness. We noted this difference in the chapter on ethics, but it is worth elaborating more on that issue.

English uses two different words, *self-interest* and *selfishness,* to distinguish between behavior that is perfectly acceptable (self-interested behavior) and behavior that is ethically inappropriate (selfish behavior). The duty of care owed to a client by his or her financial services professional requires that while it is permissible to be motivated by one's own self interest or hope for gain, the principal focus of concern for the professional is the well being of the client.

This third characteristic is embodied in the pledge mentioned above that all new CLU and ChFC (Chartered Financial Consultant) designees of The American College must make: "In all my professional relationships, I pledge myself to the following rule of ethical conduct: I shall, in light of all conditions surrounding those I serve, which I shall make every conscientious effort to ascertain and understand, render that service which, in the same circumstances, I would apply to myself."

ChFC® (Chartered Financial Consultant®) Pledge

"I shall, in light of all conditions surrounding those I serve, which I shall make every conscientious effort to ascertain and understand, render that service which, in the same circumstances, I would apply to myself."

The fourth characteristic of professionalism cited by Dr. Huebner involves a spirit of loyalty to fellow practitioners, helpfulness to the professed common cause, and disparagement of unprofessional acts that shame the profession. This means financial services professionals have a duty of care to the overall health of the financial services industry and that each professional needs to establish the profession's reputation for trust and candor. Perhaps, now more than ever, it is important for the industry to come together to assure the public, both consumers and regulatory authorities, that the industry condemns the shameful and unethical (not to mention illegal) actions performed by a few of its representatives. Part of being a professional is independently regulating one's own behavior and the actions of other members through adherence to a code of ethics. However, continued violation of the public trust will threaten this privilege and invite increased government regulation.

Requirements for a Profession

Expanding on Huebner's four basic characteristics of a professional, we can develop a list of additional requirements upon which a professional group must insist in order to be a professional in good standing. We will show how the financial services profession meets all of these requirements.

- *Body of Technical Subject Matter.* Any profession has at its core a body of subject matter which must be sufficiently technical so that the average layperson cannot readily understand it. Given the increasing complexity of financial instruments, we can see how sophisticated financial planning must become to understand and recommend complex financial instruments.

- *Academic Study.* Entrance into the profession requires mastery of the technical subject matter. Achieving this mastery requires a period of academic study. Those seeking mastery of financial services must involve themselves in a program of academic study. Further, given the fact that the financial instruments keep changing, continuing education is a necessity.

- *Entrance Barrier(s).* An individual cannot be a self-declared professional. A profession needs to have, as one of its hallmarks, a barrier to entry. This standard frequently involves examinations on the technical subject matter through which the prospective professional demonstrates his or her competence and expertise.

- *Independence.* Members of the profession must conduct their affairs in an independent manner; they must reach their judgments objectively. Financial service professionals, through detailed fact finding, apply independent judgment to their recommendations. The ability to generate income from more than one source further assures the independent nature of the advice rendered by the financial services professional.

- *Public Recognition.* There must be public recognition of the profession. Professional designations, such as LUTCF, CLU®, ChFC®, CFP® and others, have gained wide acceptance by both the public and the regulatory bodies. Members of the public have come to rely more and more upon the technical advice of financial services professionals in planning their affairs. This situation is evidenced by the high standards of ethical behavior demanded of financial services professionals and by the judicial system in cases dealing with alleged financial advisor negligence and ethical misconduct.

- *Professional Societies.* A profession needs to be guided by a society of its members. The functions of such a society include monitoring the professional actions and competence of those practicing the particular profession. There are several professional societies in any community which guide the conduct of the financial services professional. These include NAIFA, the Society of Financial Service Professionals, the CFP® Board of Standards, and other groups. Further, there is the Financial Regulatory Agency (FINRA), which has oversight on most of the behavior of financial services professionals. Finally, there is the Securities Exchange Commission (SEC) which regulates registered investment advisers and brokers dealing with securities.

- *Code of Ethics.* One way a professional society monitors the behavior of its members is through the promulgation of a code of ethics. These codes of ethics set standards of conduct for members of a profession. Such standards are set at a level that exceeds the minimum legal requirements in regard to the conduct of professional affairs. Ethical codes have been promulgated by NAIFA and The Society of Financial Service Professionals. The American College has a pledge for its CLU®, ChFC® and other designees; the LUTC program has the LUTCF® Pledge. Other organizations, such as the CFP® Board, with which a financial service professional may be affiliated, also have ethical codes. These codes set the level of professional behavior far above minimum legal standards.

Client Expectations for Professional Behavior

A client may or may not be concerned about or familiar with the characteristics of a professional which we have just mentioned. However, the client has expectations of how the professional ought to behave and looks for the hallmarks of professional behavior when dealing with financial services professionals. There are at least 10 things for which a client looks when judging whether he or she is dealing with a professional. We can capture these hallmarks of professional behavior by asking these ten questions:

1. *Does the professional listen?* Do you do all the talking? You shouldn't. Good fact finding depends on getting the client to reveal both financial and personal information. Stop and listen. Get to know the client's needs and aspirations. Obtaining this information permits you to custom-design a financial program geared to the client's specific needs and wants and not simply to what you think he or she wants.

2. *Does the professional answer my questions?* Sometimes a client will ask a question to which the answer is not immediately clear. Do not ignore the question or gloss over it. If you need to research an answer, say so. The client will respect your willingness to admit you need additional information and your commitment to searching it out.

   Sometimes clients should ask obvious questions, but they do not. Probe the clients for information. If necessary, ask if they have any questions. This will provide you with feedback on whether or not they understand their needs and the role of financial products in fulfilling those needs.

3. *Is the professional gathering sufficient information to provide good advice?* The answer will be "yes," if you are conducting a thorough fact find. The point is to be sure you have the facts before making a recommendation.

4. *Has the professional educated me about the product?* Some clients understand the intricacies of how a financial product operates, but many do not. Take the time to educate your clients on basics and on the range of available products. This way, your clients will appreciate your advice and understand what they need to purchase and why they purchased it.

5. *Has the professional taken my ability to deal with risk into consideration in making his or her recommendation?* We know that different clients regard risk differently. Many clients will reject a proposal that makes them feel uneasy because it's outside their financial comfort zone. You need to do a risk assessment. Before making a recommendation, it is good ethics and good business to find out where a client stands in this regard.

6. *Does the professional tell me about his or her designations and affiliations, and am I really dealing with someone knowledgeable?* Many of your clients are individuals you have known a short time. Many are unfamiliar with your background, but want to know more before entrusting you with financial or other highly confidential information. Some clients will ask questions in this regard. Others will remain silent, but move on if the unasked question remains unanswered.

   Provide your clients with information regarding your background. Initially, your professional business card introduces you. List your designations and other related information that indicate your status as a professional. Tell the client the professional associations to which you belong when asked. For example, "Michael Princely, LUTCF® , CLU®, ChFC®, CFP®" tells clients immediately that they are dealing with a knowledgeable individual capable of providing appropriate advice in financial matters.

7. *Does the professional provide me with a sense of steady service, or am I meeting with an individual seeking a one-time sale?* Do you return client calls? You should. Both during and after the sale, maintain contact with the client. Explain the role of periodic reviews to the client during the initial sale—then keep your promise and conduct them. Use company-approved literature to keep in touch and provide your client with current information of interest, such as pending legislation. Your client will view you as a professional with

whom a business relationship should be developed. During the recent financial crisis, one of the best things done by a number of professionals was calling each of their clients, just to find out how things were going and asking how they could be of help. Clients want professionals who care.

8. *Does the professional handle money matters properly?* Never ask the client to make a check payable to anyone other than the specific financial services company. In simpler terms, never ask the client to make out a check to you for financial products. This invites commingling of funds and represents a violation of most state laws. Keep accurate records of what monies you have collected from clients. Provide clients with the proper receipts. And, don't let checks sit in your briefcase day after day because the necessary paperwork is a hassle.

9. *Does the professional refer to other experts or is he or she intimidated by them?* Financial advisors are not accountants, attorneys or trust officers; nor is every financial advisor an expert in all financial-related fields. Clients understand this. If necessary, refer your client to a specialist. One of the most effective methods of doing this is to become part of a professional team.

Review Item: Estate Advice

Client Anne Brandon: "I don't know, Brendan, before I go ahead with these plans I would really like to talk to my accountant and see what he thinks."

Agent Brendan Malley: "I wouldn't recommend that, Anne, adding another person just confuses matters. You know, I am a little upset that you don't have enough faith me to trust that I am doing the right thing for you."

Does Agent Malley respond as a professional? Should he have responded differently?

---

10. *Does the professional seem current in his or her information?* Are you maintaining your professional skills? Many clients can sense when professionals seem out of touch with current issues. It's all well and good, for example, to obtain a professional designation, but that designation becomes worthless if your knowledge becomes outdated and irrelevant.

RESPONSIBILITIES OF PROFESSIONALISM

Having viewed the characteristics and requirements of being a professional, as well as the expectations that clients have of you as a professional, we now turn to an examination of the responsibilities of a professional. Being a professional demands increased responsibilities to your clients:

- responsibility for delivering high quality informed service to clients
- responsibility to be aware of ethical and compliance issues and to act ethically in compliance
- fiduciary responsibility

Increased Client Service

As he or she gains knowledge and experience, the financial services professional often finds that clients expect an increased level of service and expertise. Frequently, this service involves broad-based advice on technical subjects, such as retirement planning and business taxation. This means that the financial services professional must constantly seek and to improve and increase their technical knowledge.

For example, many financial services professionals engage in estate planning. In order to render advice competently about how estates should be handled, financial services professionals must be aware, among other things, of tax codes, trusts and probate laws. Much of this knowledge is interrelated to the discipline of law, and herein lies a danger for financial services professionals.

In seeking to provide clients with superior information and service, an advisor could inadvertently engage in the unauthorized practice of law. Avoid the temptation to bypass the attorney. The unauthorized practice of law opens the financial services professional to charges of ethical misconduct. This presents a dilemma for the financial services professional: namely, how to balance the demand from clients for increased technical levels of service without violating ethical codes by delving into other professional disciplines.

Here is a course of action:

- If you must give technical advice to a client, present it, as much as you can, in general terms.
- If you must give specific advice, cite sources of common knowledge. Stick to situations where the law is black-and-white, such as the nondeductibility of life insurance premiums on an

individual 1040 tax return. If the law is open to interpretation, say so and refer the client to a legal expert for an opinion. *Never draft legal documents.* If you do, you are leaving a paper trail of evidence showing ethical violations.

- Where possible, work as a member of a professional team. This team should draw professionals from a variety of disciplines. For example, a team might consist of a financial services professional, a lawyer and an accountant.

Increased Need to Be Aware of Ethical Issues

A salesperson merely sells. A professional only sells when it is in the best interest of the client. Being a professional involves a high level of trust. Clients trust you to provide the best advice for their particular situation and to look out for their best interests. These rules of trust go back to the Middle Ages. In a time period where few could read or write, clients had to rely on the ethical behavior of lawyers to draft legal documents that carried out their wishes. This ethical behavior was expected and it was enforced.

These same rules regarding professional conduct apply today. Financial services professionals must constantly bear in mind the ethical implications of their actions. Financial services professionals, in effect, must objectively judge their actions through the eyes of an unrelated third party. The prime criterion by which an action is judged is whether or not the financial services professional has acted for the welfare and benefit of the client (public) or has acted on behalf of his or her own self-interest.

LEGAL LIABILITY

Professional status confers additional responsibility in the eyes of the law. Simply stated, professionals are held to higher standards in the execution of their business duties. They are expected to have expertise and act accordingly.

They are expected to have knowledge of the law and to comply with its dictates. They are expected to place the interests of clients above their own. Under the law of torts, professionals have historically been held by the courts to higher standards of expertise and behavior than nonprofessionals.

This expectation places many financial services professionals in a situation in which they face greater legal liability than previously. The recent rash of lawsuits against the financial services companies and professionals exemplifies what can happen if financial advisors fail to act in ethical ways.

Review Item: Bothersome Paperwork
Agent Jessica Landers: "These home office rules are silly. Why should we bother keeping all these reports and illustrations? Who's going to want to look at this information years from now anyway?"
How would you respond to Agent Landers?

Lawsuits can damage reputations. They take considerable time and emotional energy. They can result in fewer leads, less selling time, and shattered careers. They can also result in high legal costs, stiff fines, and financial ruin. If you are accused of unethical and/or illegal behavior and cannot adequately support your innocence, a court may find in favor of a dissatisfied client. The key is to maximize the rewards offered by professional status and to minimize the risks of legal liability.

Practical Steps to Avoid Legal Liability

There are seven practical steps you can follow in order to enhance your reputation as a professional and to avoid legal pitfalls. They are as follows:

1. *Conduct a Compliance Audit of Written Sales Materials.* Have you been in the business 20 years? 10 years? Even if you've been in the business 5 years, you've witnessed many changes in the way financial advisors are expected to conduct their business. Yet, how often have you reviewed the written materials you are presenting to clients? In some cases, the materials are comfortable and do the job—or so you think.

   Changing company rules and client expectations are just two of the reasons for you to take the time to review your sales materials. If your company provides sales materials, make sure you are using the current versions. If you have previously developed materials, send them to your company compliance department for review before further use. Many home offices look for creative ideas and try hard to find ways of reworking materials, if necessary, so they are acceptable from a compliance standpoint.

   If you are selling securities or variable products, pay close attention to your company guidelines regarding the materials that must be provided to the client (for example, the prospectus) as well as the type of materials that you are permitted to use. For example, you may have materials in your files that are acceptable for use in the sale of a term insurance policy, but that require approval by your broker-dealer for use in the context of a variable life sale.

Be careful not to discard too much. FINRA requires that materials be maintained for a three to six year period dependant upon what they are. Check with your compliance department. Don't be tempted to throw away valuable records just to save space. Remember that problems often arise many years after a sale has taken place. If you know what type of sales materials were presented to a client, you have an indication of the potential problems that could arise. You may also have a clearer recollection of why the client made the purchase, and you're more likely to know how to go about defusing any client dissatisfaction.

2. *Conduct a Compliance Audit of Your Sales Presentations.* How do you approach a prospect? What do you say once you are in front of a prospect? Do you collect data about the client? If so, what type of materials do you use? Do you send a letter after an interview? What type of materials do you bring to a follow-up interview? Do you use illustrations? Do you follow up a sale with a letter? If so, what do you say?

   These are the types of questions you should ask yourself as you review your approach, sales, and post-sale techniques. Develop a standardized system of what you say and do. Write it down. This will provide you with documentation should problems arise at a later date.

3. *Review Licensing Requirements.* This may sound like a given. If you sell insurance, for example, take a closer look at your client list. Have a number of your key accounts moved to other states? Are you still servicing their business and selling those individuals more insurance? If so, you should investigate the licensing requirements of that second state. Given the high mobility of our society, many financial professionals are forced to maintain licensing in several states. State insurance departments often recognize this and allow for reciprocity. In other words, you don't have to sit for a second or third examination, but you do have to apply for licensing and pay the necessary fees.

   Ethical issues can unintentionally arise in this area. For example, a former resident of your state calls you. Like many early retirees from your area, she's moved to a particular mountain state. She's a long-time client and wants to obtain insurance. She needs the insurance now—not tomorrow. You stretch the residency facts as a favor and write the case. A review of the files would probably have avoided the situation. The necessary licensing in the client's new home state could have been obtained before the call.

If you deal with variable products and/or other securities, do you have the appropriate licensing? Have you taken your series 6 and series 7 exams? Have you kept your licensing up-to-date? Are you processing the business through another financial advisor who is licensed, but never sees the client? Do you justify this action because the review courses are too time-consuming? Do you feel the exam is too hard? Ethical issues can unintentionally arise in this area.

The point here is that, if you are selling variable products or mutual funds or other securities, you'll need to comply with FINRA rules and sit for the appropriate examinations. Selling these types of products without the proper licensing is both unethical and illegal. Keep in mind that inappropriate actions are widely publicized. In other words, a tarnished reputation due to a FINRA violation will be apparent to both present and potential clients. This may sound like a given. Most of you are licensed to sell insurance. Take a closer look, however, at your client list. Have a number of your key accounts moved to other states? Are you still servicing their business and selling those individuals more insurance? If so, you should investigate the licensing requirements of that second state. Generally, the address to which premium notices and other communications are sent is the determining factor in deciding which state rules apply.

4. *Pursue Continuing Education (CE).* Sales techniques evolve and change over time; so do the laws that apply to financial products. Continuing education is an excellent way to keep your knowledge base current and maintain your professional expertise. If you do not update your education continually, you may inadvertently give the wrong advice to a client.

Most agents must complete a specified number of hours of CE in order to renew their state insurance licenses. Those selling securities and variable products must also comply with tightened

FINRA rules in this regard. Try to get the most from these educational opportunities. Think carefully about what you hope to learn, what topics would broaden your abilities and where you need cutting-edge data to maintain your skills. Plot out your own tailored curriculum. This is good career planning. It will enhance your ability to provide clients with the best advice. And it will add to your reputation as a true professional within your community.

5. *Don't Overlook Documentation.* Many of us hate paperwork. Unfortunately, it's no excuse when dealing with a client complaint or a lawsuit. Take the time to document your activities. Once you have reviewed both the written materials you use and the sales practices you employ, set up a system that makes it easy to pinpoint your actions.

   For example, documentation should include placing a signed copy of the illustrative material used to sell a product in each client's file. It might also include the drafting and retention of a follow-up letter outlining what was sold and for what purpose(s). Documentation can also help your sales effort by making you more cognizant of what you are doing and why.

6. *Maintain Errors and Omissions (E&O) Coverage.* The complexities of today's products, coupled with the rapid changes in our economy, mean that even the soundest recommendation can turn sour. A financial product can fail to perform as expected. There is always risk in investment. A client, despite education and periodic servicing, may choose to forget that he or she was told that.

   Consequently, all financial services professionals should maintain E&O coverage. This coverage typically provides excellent legal counsel and helps to defray the costs involved in defending your actions and reputation in a lawsuit. Without E&O coverage, you risk both your property and your career.

   E&O coverage has its limitations. For example, it will not protect you in situations of intentional deceit and fraud. It will, however, enable you to present your side of a case properly. Coupled with our other suggestions, E&O coverage enables you to launch a defense, which demonstrates that you have behaved in both a legal and an ethical manner.

   Many of you already maintain E&O coverage. It is provided to you through your company or may be available through your professional association. Examine the terms of the policy. They'll provide you with additional guidance in the conduct of your career. For example, your company-provided policy might cover you only in sales situations involving inhouse products. If you're a captive agent and outside sales are not permitted, the terms of the policy serve as a further warning of your obligation to live by the terms of your contract. If you're permitted to sell or broker other products, the terms of your current policy may indicate a need to obtain supplementary coverage. The risks are too great to your family, your property, and your career to conduct any sale without the protection of E&O coverage. Take a few minutes to determine if you are covered, and the extent to which you are covered.

7. *Provide Clients with Good Service.* It's easier to avoid a problem than to solve a problem. This statement is particularly true when it comes to issues of ethics and marketplace practices. Providing your clients with good service at the time of the initial encounter and possible sale is a big step in the right direction. Periodic reviews (a process that continues this good service) are crucial in preventing trouble.

Satisfied clients enhance your reputation and improve your business. Financial advisors who perform needs selling, who maintain regular contact, and who keep their clients fully informed about product performance are taking three key steps to prevent ethics-related problems before they arise.

Attributes of Professional Behavior

We can conclude that a professional is an individual with a high level of knowledge and expertise on a technical subject, who needs to adhere to high ethical standards in the application of this knowledge and expertise. Although these criteria may sound like an onerous burden, they are not when one considers the gains. The financial services professional has achieved a role as a member of the profession. This creates opportunity for increased service. It also provides increased business rewards. Once again, good ethics and good business go hand-in-hand.

PROFESSIONAL CODES OF ETHICS

Professionals take the law seriously, but they also take the law as a starting point in guiding their actions. Between the positive law and the unwritten ethical laws are codes of ethics.

The fourth criteria of Dr. Huebner was a spirit of loyalty to other professionals, helpfulness to the common cause and the forbiddance of unprofessional acts to shame the profession. The most useful guide in their enterprise are codes of ethics.

Codes of ethics have been developed to provide professionals with ethical rules and working guidelines that go beyond the law. These codes offer a series of guidelines for work-related decision-making. The codes also serve to standardize public and professional expectations. Finally, codes of ethics aid professionals in reaching the level of trust that the public has come to expect.

Codes Applicable to the Financial Services Professional

Financial services professionals are fortunate in that they have a variety of organizations dedicated to their professional needs. These organizations are aware of the increasing ethical pressures on their members. In response, they have drafted professional pledges and codes of conduct. Among the pledges and codes applicable to the financial services professional are the following:

- LUTCF Pledge
- NAIFA Code of Ethics
- The American College Code of Ethics
- Society of Financial Service Professionals Code of Ethics
- The Million Dollar Round Table Code of Ethics
- The CFP® Code of Ethics

Common Themes among Professional Codes

There is no need to feel overwhelmed by the number of pledges and ethical codes that apply to them. They should be looked upon as reference devices. Relying on a number of sources, rather than relying on just one, is a means of assurance. Most codes rest on ethical common sense and share seven common themes:

- Every code calls on professionals to look out for the best interests of the client before their own.
- Most of the codes, in one way or another, ask the professionals to conduct themselves with fairness, objectivity, honesty and integrity.
- Each code requires the professionals to protect the confidential information of the clients.
- Most codes require that the professional present sufficient information, enough to allow the client to make an informed decision.
- Each requires the professionals to continue the learning process throughout their careers.
- Each code asks professionals to conduct themselves in such a way as to bring honor to themselves and to their professions.
- Most of the codes specify that the financial services professionals should comply with the law.

These common themes and sentiments should strike you as common sense. You are urged to study these codes and take them seriously. They will serve as strong guideposts to your professional development and achievement.

Knowledge of the codes and their common themes can enable you to better deal with the complexities of today's marketplace. They can provide a barometer of what is expected of you by your profession and by the public. They are not a substitute for the law. They are meant to act as a supplement to the law. Often they go beyond the law in providing guidelines for ethical behavior—guidelines that, in turn, translate into sound business practices.

1. First and foremost in each code is the requirement to put the client's interest before one's own. The Million Dollar Round Table Code states that members shall "always place the best interests of their clients above their own direct or indirect interests." Your role is to serve your client, even if that means setting aside your interests

2. The codes also insist on fairness, honesty, objectivity and integrity. The code of the Society of Financial Service Professionals has canons that deal with "fairness" and "integrity." *Fairness* means giving everyone his or her due, and integrity means being honest and true to oneself. *Objectivity* means that habit of mind that allows one to step back from a situation in order to make a judgment from a disinterested perspective. It involves avoiding conflicts of interest; in particular, avoiding giving in to the financial advisor's self-interest, and giving the client's interest due weight. These characteristics are the basic virtues of the ethical person.

3. The third provision found in each code lays out the requirement of confidentiality. The NAIFA code puts it succinctly. It is the professional's responsibility "to maintain the client's confidences."

4. The fourth provision, found in several codes, is the requirement to disclose the information necessary for the client to make an informed decision. The MDRT code states that members shall "make full and adequate disclosures of all facts necessary to enable their clients to make informed decisions." The NAIFA code cites the responsibility "to present accurately and honestly all facts essential to clients' decisions."

5. The next provision deals with competence and continuing education. The American College Code, Canon IV, calls on the professional "to continue your studies throughout your working life so as to maintain a high level of professional competence." NAIFA's code calls on the financial advisor "to perfect skills and increase knowledge through continuing education," while MDRT insists members shall "maintain the highest standards of competence . . . and improve professional knowledge, skills, and competence."

Clients expect sound and accurate recommendations. Clients can be harmed by incompetent advice. Agents can be harmed when they provide it. These factors demonstrate the need for financial services professionals to keep abreast of changes in their field. The NAIC has long recognized this need and has strongly backed continuing education requirements. The following guidelines constitute the most basic requirements of the industry's codes.

Why Continuing Education is Important

1. To maintain competence, it is important to admit your lack of expertise. If you are involved in a case that requires expertise that you lack, call on an expert. The client will respect you and appreciate the expert advice.

2. All the codes require behavior that brings honor to individuals and the profession. NAIFA cites a responsibility "to address professional standards of conduct . . . to help raise the professional standards." The MDRT requires a member to "maintain personal conduct which will reflect favorably . . . on the industry."

3. The codes specify that the professional should comply with the law. The MDRT code puts it this way, "abide by and conform to all provisions of the laws and regulations in the jurisdictions in which they do business." As we have seen, it is an important ethical obligation to abide by all just laws, because the laws are society's rule to help achieve the common good.

The Code of Ethics and Professional Responsibility adopted by the Certified Financial Planner Board of Standards presents these provisions in a slightly different way. It offers seven principles that cite the character traits the CFP® should possess: integrity, objectivity, competence, fairness, confidentiality, professionalism, and diligence. What the seven principles require is that the CFP® designee offer services with integrity and honesty, not misrepresenting products, and treating all stakeholders fairly. The service should be competent and diligent—that is, prompt and thorough. Decisions should be made with objectivity, which requires putting the client's needs to the forefront and, in a professional manner, always respecting the client's confidentiality.

PRACTICAL APPLICATION

What do these codes mean in terms of daily professional practice? The American College pledge says, "I shall ... render that service which ... I would apply to myself." The Society's code calls for putting the client's interest before one's own, and the CFP® code calls for the practitioner to act "in the interest of the client." Though not identical, all mandate something like the Golden Rule, "Do unto others as you would have them do unto you."

To offer a client the same thorough attention to detail that a financial services professional would apply to an investment for himself or herself is no small requirement. Think about the kind of service a planner would give to himself or herself or to close relatives or friends. The planner would make absolutely certain to understand all the apparent and hidden costs. The planner would want to know how much it would cost now and whether the cost over the life of the product would be fixed or variable. The planner would want to understand clearly the potential risks of the investment or insurance policy. If it is an interest-sensitive product, is the financial advisor (or the client) able to monitor the financial stability of the product regularly? What are the costs of withdrawal? Does the financial advisor understand the potential benefits of the product in the short term, as well as in the long term? Does he or she know exactly how to maximize those benefits or what actions to take to reduce the potential harms? The professional would not go into an investment or insurance policy purchase without making use of as much knowledge about the product as he or she was able to acquire responsibly.

The professional may believe that the client has a particularly strong interest in knowing all the professional details; however, some clients simply are not interested in all those details. One of the benefits of being in the financial services business is that the planner has access to information and knowledge that the general public does not have. But the advisor relationship requires that he or she make that knowledge available to help the client make better-informed investment decisions. Rendering the service to clients that he or she would expect for him- or herself requires the professional's responsibility to present the information in a way that clients can understand and use in their decision making.

Of course, a professional cannot force someone to understand something, and a client may not even want to know all the details. Nonetheless, it is the financial services professional's obligation to provide the client with the needed information and to present this information in a manner that the client can understand. The professional should help the client understand why he or she needs the information about the product and what its financial effect will be in the short and long terms.

Client-Focused Service

Most codes also stipulate that the financial services professional take into account the conditions surrounding the client and, as The American College pledge requires, "shall make every conscientious effort to ascertain and understand" such conditions. This means one cannot simply "sell off" products and be a salesperson. There must be consultative or client-focused planning or selling. Such an approach requires the financial services professional to gather as much information as possible from the client about needs, goals, interests and assets in order to put together an investment package that will best meet the client's needs.

The sale of products is essentially client-driven. The financial advisor must approach the client with a willingness to listen carefully. The client can best provide the information regarding his or her own needs and goals. The client may also think that he or she knows what product best fits those needs and will help him or her achieve their financial objectives, but the professional should keep the client focused on articulating needs and goals in order to recommend the most suitable product.

Agent of the Client

Consultative financial advising is a sound approach to building good relationships with clients. But what is this relationship to the client? Many claim it is a fiduciary relationship. In a previous chapter, we looked at the financial services professional when he or she was an agent of a company. But the role of the professional is more complicated that that. The independent agent is clearly the agent of the client. The professional who is contracted to a company usually has the dual role of agent for a financial services company and agent for the client. As the agent of the company, he or she is expected to accurately represent to the client the products or services sold by the company and the costs and benefits, as well as to act on behalf of the company. Not many financial services companies still have exclusive relationships with financial advisors, so while financial advisors' loyalty is a concern, the financial services professional is usually not required to sell only the policies of one or two companies. Most who deal primarily with the products of one company feel that their obligation to the company is to consider those products first to meet client needs, and then go outside, only if an appropriate policy or investment is not available within that company.

This traditional approach serves several purposes. First, the advisor is able to gain in-depth knowledge of the products of one or two companies, which would be nearly impossible if a person tried to cover all the products on the market. This knowledge enables the professional to serve the client better. Second, it saves the financial services professional extensive research time to be able to work from a body of familiar products. Of course, in some instances, this could be detrimental to a client who needs more extensive research to find just the right product. It is important for the professional to honestly inform the client of his or her primary relationship with a particular company. The client should understand that these products are the ones the planner will research and present in most cases. It is deceptive and clearly unethical to fail to disclose that primary relationship.

Review Item: Dual Loyalty Agent
Agent Albert has a contract with his primary company that is promoting a new product and expecting him to meet certain sales quotas. He does not feel this is the best product for a number of his clients and wants to sell them a product from another company. However, he will get in trouble with his manager if he does.
Consider Agent Albert's situation. Do you have any comments? Does this present any ethical or legal issues?

The financial services professional is also an agent for the client. The client trusts the agent with confidential information. It is important to note that courts have increasingly found that the common law understanding of the word agent is "agent of the client." Courts have held that, when a financial services professional induces reliance on his or her expertise, that person incurs liability for decisions made on the basis of that expertise. When a financial advisor says to a client, "I am your agent," the planner does indeed take on the responsibilities and liabilities of an agent of the client.

Many educators, speakers and managers stress the importance of selling a financial service or product solely on the basis of client need. Selling on any other basis, such as the needs and interests of the salesperson, the sales manager, or the company, makes no sense in the long term. The salesperson may be persuasive enough to make fast sales in order to meet a bonus deadline, or the company may be promoting a particular product with higher commission rates. But unless the product really meets the needs of the client over the long term, that client will not keep up the payments, which eventually costs the company money. Clients who feel they were sold products that did not meet their needs are not likely to become repeat customers.

Review Item: Professional?

Agent Hennessy to Agent Clinton: "I worked really hard to get those designations and there is no way that I am going to take any continuing education class that is actually going to make me work! There are plenty of easy classes online that I can take and not have to think much about."

What do you think of the agent's attitude? Does it exemplify the attitude of a true professional? Why or why not?

A client will not refer friends and relatives to a salesperson if the client does not believe in the salesperson's ability to listen carefully and respond. So, while the short-term sales may look good, the long-term financial position of the salesperson, the selling agency and the selling company are hurt by any sales that do not meet client needs. The same arguments, of course, support continuing attention to the changing needs of clients over time.

In summary, it is both ethically required and financially wise for the financial services professional to thoroughly understand the client's needs and act to fulfill those needs as much as possible. This approach is further corroborated by the Code of Ethics of the Society of Financial Service Professionals.

PROFESSIONAL COMPETITIVE INTEGRITY

We have mentioned that each code requires personal conduct that brings honor to the profession, including treating other professionals with respect. The link between the financial services professional and the industry as a whole is of particular importance when speaking of competing companies and financial advisors. Too often, advisors have separated themselves from the industry. They speak of their products and their companies as if these elements were totally separate and apart from the industry. They do not see the importance of working diligently to build and maintain consumer trust in the financial services industry as a whole, and undercut this trust by making disparaging remarks about other companies.

The rule here is to avoid making negative comments or insinuations about other companies or the industry in general. Not only is it poor ethics and a violation of professional responsibilities, it may be illegal. For example, many state insurance regulations prohibit the use of impaired financial status of a competitor as a tool to make new sales. It is also important to be very careful in making comparisons between your product and the product of another company. You should always rely on the marketing literature and information supplied by your company. If necessary, get help from the competitive unit at your home office in preparing a comparison.

Here is one final note of caution: Many financial services professionals work for more than one carrier over the course of a career. They become familiar with each company's products and operations. They develop their own opinions as to where each company is superior. Sometimes, these opinions can lead to ethical and legal troubles. Be sure to review the agency agreements you have signed with your prior carrier(s) and your current carrier. Be careful not to violate any provisions regarding the transfer of business from a prior carrier.

Don't move clients from one carrier to another unless it is clearly in their best interests. No client likes to think he or she bought the wrong product. If you place doubt in a client's mind about a prior decision, you are likely to place doubt in the client's mind as to the wisdom of your current recommendation.

Summary of Professional Responsibilities

Insurance and financial advisors are increasingly gaining public recognition as professionals. With this recognition comes both status and additional responsibility. Advisors now face higher standards of behavior and service. They face increased liability. They also face far greater opportunities.

Become aware of the laws that apply to your practice. Ignorance of the law is no defense, either ethically or legally. It is important to assume responsibility for your career growth and not to rely solely on company training to provide you with the newest ideas or the freshest techniques. Participate in recognized continuing education programs and look at these requirements as an opportunity to grow both your business and your skills.

Follow the guidelines found in the industry's professional codes. They will encourage integrity, disclosure and honest dealings with your clients.

Review Item: Striving for Professionalism?
Agent Jenny Mayfair: "I've just completed my licensing. What more can I do for my clients to see me as a true professional?"
How would you answer Agent Mayfair's question?

Educate your clients about your products. Make sure they understand the type of product(s) they are buying and the reasons behind their purchase(s).

Conduct periodic reviews. They will serve to reeducate your clients on the reasons for their purchases, as well as on the process to uncover new needs.

Document your activities. The documentation may protect you in the case of legal action. The documentation will also help to make you more cognizant of what you are doing and why.

Refer to other professionals when needed. Do not attempt to feign knowledge or expertise. Become part of the client's advisory team. Leverage the influence of other professionals to accomplish the client's goals.

Strive to create and maintain a positive public image in your community not only of yourself, but of the industry. Doing all of these things is both good ethics and good business.

Financial services advisors have achieved public recognition as professionals. People want to deal with ethical individuals. They want to trust those with whom they conduct business. Those who engage in deceitful practices may close sales in the short run, but it is ethical financial advisors who ultimately build practices.

CHAPTER REVIEW QUESTIONS

Answers to Review Questions are in the Appendix.

1. Which of the following is one of the seven basic requirements for a discipline to be considered a profession?

   (A) Members of the profession must earn above a standard minimum level of income.
   (B) Members of the profession cannot be self-declared as professionals.
   (C) Members of the profession must hold a postgraduate degree from an accredited university.
   (D) Members of the profession cannot enter the profession prior to a completion of a 7-year apprenticeship and successful completion of written examinations.

2. The text advises that financial services professionals must be aware of knowledge that is interrelated to the discipline of law. Consequently, in order to disperse this information properly

   (A) an insured financial advisor is exempt from rules regarding the unauthorized practice of law
   (B) attorneys are covered by rules forbidding the unauthorized practice of insurance-related advice
   (C) technical advice to clients should be specific in nature
   (D) technical advice to clients should be given in general terms

3. Under the law of torts, professionals

   (A) are exempt from actions regarding bodily harm
   (B) are exempt from standards of expertise due to their certified credentials
   (C) have historically been held to higher standards of expertise and behavior than nonprofessionals
   (D) have historically been held to lower standards of expertise and behavior than nonprofessionals

4. How does the text suggest you handle requests from clients for specific tax advice or legal matters?

   (A) Refer your client to the appropriate specialist.
   (B) First try to draft the requested documents yourself.
   (C) Provide your client with doctored home-office prototype documents.
   (D) Do not let the client call on the expertise of another professional.

5. A code of ethics establishes which of the following for members of a profession?

   (A) rules of law
   (B) statutes of state
   (C) standards of conduct
   (D) rules of etiquette

READ THE FOLLOWING DIRECTIONS BEFORE CONTINUING

The questions below differ from the preceding questions in that they all contain the word EXCEPT. So you understand fully the basis used in selecting each answer, be sure to read each question carefully.

6. All of the following are requirements of a profession EXCEPT

   (A) any profession has at its core a body of subject matter
   (B) entrance into the profession requires mastery of the technical subject matter
   (C) a profession has as one of its hallmarks no barriers to entry
   (D) members of the profession must conduct their affairs in an independent manner

7. All of the following are among the codes of ethics applicable to the financial services professional EXCEPT

   (A) the NAIC Code of Ethics
   (B) The American College Code of Ethics
   (C) the Society of Financial Service Professionals Code of Ethics
   (D) the CFP® Code of Ethics

8. All of the following are practical steps that financial services professionals can use to avoid legal liability EXCEPT

   (A) Conduct a compliance audit of written sales materials.
   (B) Conduct a compliance audit of your sales presentations.
   (C) Overlook unnecessary documentation.
   (D) Review licensing requirements.

9. As stated in the text, being a professional carries with it all of the following EXCEPT

   (A) increased demands for service by clients
   (B) increased risk of legal liability
   (C) increased paperwork
   (D) increased need to be aware of ethical issues

10. Clients ask themselves each of the following questions when judging whether or not they are dealing with a professional EXCEPT

    (A) Does the professional listen?
    (B) Does the professional ask me questions?
    (C) Has the professional educated me about the product?
    (D) Does the professional handle money matters properly?

Learning Objectives

An understanding of the material in this chapter should enable the student to

1. Identify a six-step procedure financial services professionals can use to implement the FINRA/NASD Rules of Fair Dealing into their practices.

2. Identify the factors that a prospective investor should consider before investing.

3. List and explain the four types of risks.

4. Explain the concept of risk tolerance and risk tolerance assessment techniques.

5. Describe the categories of investments.

6. Identify the characteristics of investment diversification within the context of risk management.

7. Describe the FINRA/NASD Conduct Rules.

WHY ETHICAL MARKETING PRACTICES ARE IMPORTANT

How should a financial services professional behave? Which practices should be followed and which avoided? Is rebating OK? When is replacement of an insurance policy acceptable? What are the limits on how one should advertise? The purpose of this chapter is to examine various practices of financial services professionals to determine which are acceptable and which are not.

Ethical behavior is important, because clients' viewpoints of the financial services industry are shaped by their experiences with an individual financial planner or insurance agent. Positive experiences lead to a respect for the professional and the industry. Negative experiences do great harm to the planner's and the industry's reputations.

Dissatisfied clients speak to friends, neighbors and acquaintances about their poor experiences, thus spreading a negative image of the industry. Dissatisfied clients can also bring the situation to the attention of the Securities and Exchange Commission or state insurance commissioners. A poor public image of a profession creates difficulties for its participants.

Dissatisfied clients don't welcome financial services professionals warmly. Recommendations of products are met with an air of skepticism. Regulatory authorities respond by tightening current rules or imposing new ones. The financial services industry then loses flexibility in doing business. An individual responsible for client dissatisfaction is likely to lose the dissatisfied client's business. There may be a charge back against commission income. Referrals are lost, the professional's reputation is tarnished, and future career opportunities may be closed. Poor marketing ethics hurt the agent, the company and the industry.

Recent malpractice suits make it clear that there are two areas in which agents are held accountable—suitability (providing suitable products) and disclosure (failure to give sufficient disclosure). The professional pledge taken by CLUs to "look out for the best interest of the client" obliges the agent to find a suitable policy to fill the needs of the client. This requires that the agent has the competence to ascertain which policies or products best suit the client's needs, as well as the willpower or moral fiber to overcome the lure of recommending a less suitable policy that pays a higher commission. Meeting the suitability requirement also necessitates that agents "learn enough to maintain their level of competence."

We will discuss the practices that a financial services professional needs to observe in the processes of dealing fairly with clients. We will use NAIC model laws and FINRA/NASD conduct rules as our guide in determining what is required.

In the chapter on the legal framework, we saw there are two sources that articulate proper conduct for financial services professionals—the NAIC model laws and the FINRA/NASD conduct rules. The NAIC sets out the objective of fair, just and equitable treatment of policyowners and claimants. As part of its work, the NAIC drafts model laws in the fields of life and health insurance. Today, there are over 600 model laws and regulations. Five of these model laws are of particular interest in determining which practices financial services professionals should follow. These models are the

- rules governing the advertising of life insurance
- life insurance and annuities replacement model regulation
- life insurance illustrations model regulation
- life insurance disclosure model regulation
- unfair trade practices act

These five models, broadly adopted by the states, establish marketing and disclosure standards for insurance agents. They prohibit defamation and false advertising. The models give insurance commissioners substantial powers to investigate both carriers and agents suspected of violations. Punishments for violations include fines as well as license suspension and revocation. These regulations provide guidelines for the appropriate practice of financial services professionals. They can be supplemented by the set of guidelines for ethical practice found in The Financial Industry Regulatory Authority's Rules of Conduct.[26] The essence of ethical conduct for the FINRA/NASD is fair dealing.

FAIR DEALING

Fair dealing requires several things:

1. There must be an effort to clearly understand the client's current financial condition.
2. There must be an effort to understand the client's investment objectives. In some cases, this involves educating a client and helping the client clarify his or her needs.
3. There must be an application of the professional's expertise to develop strategies to meet those needs and goals. Sometimes, there will be one clear strategy. In many situations, however, more than one strategy is possible. It then becomes the job of the representative to explain to and, if necessary, educate the client on the pros and cons of the various proposed alternatives.
4. There must be a consideration of the suitability of the various strategies to meet the client's needs. Determining suitable products to accommodate needs is extremely important.

---

26. FINRA/NASD Manual Section on Conduct Rules 2000-3410.

5. Professionals should only recommend or sell products the client needs. For example, a high-risk strategy of funding college tuition for a newborn might be suitable for a young marketing director, but might involve too much risk for a middle-aged engineer who is starting a second family.

6. Finally, there must be periodic reviews because client's needs do not remain static.

The first four of these professional obligations have to do with suitability requirements, which we will examine more thoroughly. The fifth has to do with ethical sales of products, which we will look at presently. To begin then, it is clear that if a professional is to look out for the client's best interests, he or she should determine which products are suitable for a client, starting with ascertaining the client's current financial condition.

Understand the Client's Current Financial Condition

To ascertain the client's current financial condition, it is necessary to introduce a fact-finding process. This involves asking questions such as: How much household income is being earned? If the client is married, do both spouses work? How much income does each spouse earn? Are there substantial liabilities, such as a home mortgage? Are there smaller credit card debts leading to recurring monthly bills? Are there other sources of income? For example, does the client own rental property? Has the client received an inheritance that has been invested?

Fact finding involves more than just multiplying an annual salary by a predetermined number of years. It is more than looking at a "guesstimated" set of expenses, extrapolating them against future income, and rounding out a shortfall on a yellow pad. Fact finding should be thorough. It must take into consideration both financial and non-financial information. It should also take into consideration other financial needs aside from life insurance. For example, a thorough fact find might uncover deficiencies in a client's disability income protection. Fact finding is also critical when dealing with business owners.

Other key financial factors that will be uncovered through fact finding include ownership of life insurance and investment experience. Has the client ever purchased life insurance before? If so, when and what type? Does the client understand and appreciate the various insurance products being offered in the marketplace? Has the client previously made investment in individual stocks or mutual funds? If so, what type of stocks or funds? Were they conservative or aggressive in nature? Did the client select these securities on his or her own initiative, or was the investment based on professional advice? Does the client own shares in a real estate investment trust (REIT) or own real estate as an investment property?

It takes hard work to assemble all pertinent facts about the client. In addition, these factors must be considered for each member of the client's family unit. For example, the client may have substantial assets, but have an adult child who suffers from a disability, making future work impossible. Such a situation affects the client's overall financial needs and estate plan.

Understand the Client's Investment Objectives

After determining the client's financial condition, the professional needs to find out what goals the client wishes to accomplish. The fact-finding process should uncover the client's financial goals and investment objectives. Some common financial goals might include a desire to pay off a 30-year mortgage before retirement, save for college tuition or have the means to opt for early retirement. Lately, some advisors have even begun to investigate the quality of life goals. What else, besides security, is the client interested in? For example, is the client interested in giving to charitable causes?

The fact-finding process should provide you with other pieces of financial information that are important to the development of any financial plan. Key factors would include the client's time horizon. For example, how many years will elapse before the client's child enters college? By early retirement, does the client mean age 50 or age 60? Does the client wish to pay off the mortgage in 5 years, 15 years or have payoff coincide with a retirement date?

Applying Professional Expertise to Facts to Develop Strategies

A further aspect of fair dealing involves the application of the agent's professional knowledge and expertise to the data to develop strategies that will meet the client's needs. For some prospects, an analysis will indicate that insurance is part of the solution. In other cases, investment vehicles, such as annuities or mutual funds, will form part of the solution.

Whether your recommendation involves insurance or an investment vehicle, it is important to remember that the product should be appropriate for the particular client. One size does not fit all. The central question is: Does the recommended product meet the client's needs, financial abilities and personal risk profile?

Determining Suitability

The steps mentioned above are essential in trying to meet the demands of suitability. We need to examine the client's needs and objectives and recommend products and strategies that suit those needs. Determining suitability is difficult. It is the end result of doing the research and fact finding to determine the client's financial condition, identifying the client's objectives, and developing strategies to meet those objectives. It is determining whether those strategies really fit the objectives and needs. We have given a detailed account of Suitability Rule 2310 in a prior chapter. FINRA/NASD conduct rules require that financial professionals make reasonable efforts to obtain information about the customer's financial status, tax status, investment objectives and other information to be used in making recommendations.

The Importance of Selling Suitable Products

There has been a great deal of discussion regarding the difference between the obligations which broker-dealers and registered investment advisors (RIAs) have to their clients and whether the general public understands these differences. Registered investment advisers are held to a fiduciary standard, while broker-dealers have a less stringent obligation to recommend suitable products. The question of when a broker should be held to a fiduciary standard is an important one. However, what is beyond dispute is that, whatever additional duties one may have, every financial services professional has an obligation to recommend only suitable products to his or her clients.

Suitable products are products which are not only appropriate in terms of the client's stated goals and objectives, but also remain appropriate when considered in context with the client's circumstances and overall financial health. For example, an Equity Indexed Annuity may be an appropriate product for someone who is looking to secure a steady stream of income without having any immediate need for cash. However, an EIA may not be an appropriate product if the client lacks additional, more liquid assets in case of a financial emergency. Therefore, it is important to keep in mind that it is nearly impossible to recommend a suitable product for a client or potential client without understanding and keeping abreast of the changes in his or her life and the lives of family members and other dependents.

The responsibility of financial services professionals to recommend only suitable products results from the trust that is placed in them by their clients. As we mentioned, financial services professionals are not simply sales persons, and a more robust standard than caveat emptor should apply in their relationships with their clients. This is the case because of the relative expertise of the financial services professional, the vulnerability of the client in terms of lack of information and the expertise and importance of the asset with which the financial services professional is engaged to assist, which is the client's overall financial health and security.

RISK

One of the most important aspects of suitability is determining the client's risk tolerance. Is the client aware of his or her risk profile? Is the client aggressive, moderate or risk-averse (conservative)? Ethical issues can arise if a client is sold a type of product that carries a greater degree of risk than is indicated by the client's risk profile. This means that one of the important obligations of an advisor is to educate the client about risk, risk tolerance and how to conduct risk management. Let's look at those three factors:

- investment risk
- risk tolerance
- risk management

A financial services professional can typically offer clients greater product selection than was available 20 years ago—or even 5 years ago. A myriad of available products offer everything from term insurance to highly speculative securities. The broad choice of product offerings permits clients to tailor their programs more than ever before. This variety, however, comes at the price of fewer guarantees. In most cases, a greater proportion of the investment risk inherent in the product is now borne by clients. More and more the question will be: Was the consumer sold an appropriate or suitable product? Failure to answer this question in the affirmative can be an invitation to a lawsuit. None of us wants to be involved in a lawsuit, and we all want to do the right thing when it comes to providing our clients with service. With increased product choice, we'll have to consider not only how the product meets a client's needs but also how that product matches the client's ability to handle risk. This raises two questions:

- Does the client understand investment risk?
- How does one determine the client's risk tolerance?

Good Ethics
Good ethics and good marketplace practices indicate that agents assume most clients are risk-averse.

INVESTMENT RISK

Overview of Investment Considerations

Individuals have many choices with regard to the investment of their money. In helping your clients achieve their financial goals, it is likely that you will spend some time discussing alternative savings and investment vehicles. As you do, there are seven factors of which you should make your clients aware.

Seven Investment Decision Factors

The seven factors that clients should consider are:

1. *Risk-Reward Trade-Off.* Financial savings and investment vehicles need to be considered in light of both risk and reward. Some investments carry more risk than others. Generally, an investment that offers the potential of greater return carries greater risk. Due to the proliferation of today's sophisticated products, this is a factor that must be considered by clients.

   For example, it is true that cash values may increase at a faster rate within a variable product if the stock market soars; ultimately equating to fewer premium payments and/or greater coverage. However, it is also true that poor stock market results may cause more premiums to be paid at higher rates, in comparison to a traditional life insurance product.

2. *Timing of Return.* The dates of some investment returns are easier to pinpoint than others. For example, it's relatively easy to pinpoint when interest will be paid in a certificate of deposit. In general, the easier it is to pinpoint the date of return, the lower the investment risk. In general, the lower the investment risk, the lower the potential reward.

   For example, a real estate investment might offer the potential of substantial appreciation, but the exact amount and timing of this appreciation is not easily determined. Applying this to an insurance product, we can see that a traditional product offers far more predictability with regard to what is due (premiums) and what will be paid (face value).

3. *Tax Consequences*. Some investments offer tax benefits; others do not. For example, interest earned on a certificate of deposit is taxed at regular income tax rates. Appreciation realized on a long-term real estate investment would, in contrast, be eligible for more favorable capital gains rates.

   Similarly, most clients need to be made aware of preferred tax treatment of life insurance. While not the main benefit of the product, tax deferral offers the opportunity for capital accumulation at a more accelerated rate than would otherwise be possible.

4. *Liquidity*. Some investments can be more like cash than others. If one needs quick access to money, liquidity becomes an important factor. For example, a money market account is a highly liquid investment. In many cases, an individual can write a check against these savings without notifying anyone or waiting for any sale of underlying investments.

5. *Marketability*. Some assets can be sold and converted into cash more easily than others. Like liquidity, this becomes an important factor for any client who believes he or she will need to tap their investments quickly to satisfy potential liabilities. For example, stock can be sold relatively quickly through the operation of the exchanges that match buyers and sellers. Dollars can be received within a matter of days. A real estate investment, on the other hand, might take months or years to convert to cash.

   Marketability is an important factor in developing client financial plans. If clients hold assets that are relatively illiquid and/or for which there is a limited market (for example, a small business), life insurance can provide needed dollars to enable the family to avoid a low-priced fire sale.

6. *Required Management and Supervision*. Some investments require relatively little management or supervision and clients remain fairly passive, merely waiting for their returns. A certificate of deposit or mutual fund are two such examples. Other investments require far more hands-on management and supervision.

   For example, rental real estate might require the investors to obtain tenants, make repairs and personally collect rents. Some clients have the time and expertise needed to make such an enterprise successful; others do not. Even those clients who have the time and expertise may not wish to devote them to a particular project.

It is important to remember that not all investments require your client to devote the same amount of time or to have the same level of expertise. In general, more risky investments offering potentially greater returns require more management and supervision. With regard to insurance, think of these factors in terms of a potential product mix.

For example, older clients, who several years ago purchased a variable universal life policy, may become concerned if premium dollars are fully allocated into aggressive subaccounts. These clients may choose to reduce their risk exposure by electing a more conservative subaccount mix, which is an example of management and policy supervision.

7. *Diversification.* In reviewing any financial plan, it is important to consider the role of diversification. Simply stated, clients should not have all of their money in the same place. Clients should spread their risk by spreading money over various investments. With regard to an insurance plan, consider the situation of a highly leveraged client with one or two investment assets. This may sound far fetched, but how many of your clients carry heavy mortgages on their major asset(s)? Insurance can help to even out this situation by reducing risk in the event of premature death. In other words, a forced sale can be averted because the funds will be there. (We will discuss diversification more thoroughly later in this chapter.)

Consider referencing these seven factors any time you design a plan. They are one way of introducing the concept of investment risk and the need for planning. Some clients—usually those who would consider themselves the most conservative—have difficulty realizing that all financial plans carry an element of risk. Recognizing risk is the first step in determining how to manage it. Alerting your clients to these factors is both an example of good ethics and good business practices.

TYPES OF INVESTMENT RISK

What is investment risk? Many people equate investment risk with loss of principal. The seven investment consideration factors can be used to show your client that investment risk involves more than just the loss of principal.

There are four major categories of investment risk that your clients should consider: market risk, interest rate risk, inflation risk (purchasing power risk), and default risk.

Investment Brew
A recipe for an "Investment Brew" includes: • risk reward trade off   • timing of return   • tax consequences   • liquidity   • marketability   • required management and supervision   • diversification

Market Risk

This involves the loss of money due to a general downward business cycle. For example, clients who invested in publicly-traded stock in 1987 suffered losses as the market crashed. It was not just the stock of one company that suffered, but stocks across the entire board. Those who invested in the early and late 1990s. These were counter-balanced, however, by subsequent stock market gains, only to experience sharp market declines beginning in April of 2000 and again in 2008. Those who invested in hedge funds based on sub-prime mortgages in the latter part of the first decade of the 21st century faced losses. It is important to educate clients on market risk because so many of today's financial instruments are based on separate accounts that reflect market gains and losses.

Clients who understand the concept of market risk are able to anticipate the fact that a bull market can become a bear market. They have a better appreciation of the role played by traditional products that offer guaranteed returns, and of your role as a financial services professional.

Interest Rate Risk

This reflects the fact that an investment with a fixed interest rate is worth less if interest rates rise above the guaranteed amount. For example, an individual who purchases a 10-year bond issued by the federal government at 3.5 percent will suffer a loss if he or she must sell that bond before the maturity date, when current interest rates are at 6 percent. The reverse is also true. An investment with a guaranteed rate rises in value as current interest rates fall.

Many of your clients may not have bond holdings, but they may be familiar with the concept of interest rate risk through their adjustable rate mortgages. If rates fall, their mortgage payments fall. On the other hand, if rates rise, their mortgage payments ratchet up. Uncovering this type of information as part of your fact finding will enable you to better advise your clients.

Inflation Risk

The next major category of risk to which your clients should be alerted is inflation risk. Sometimes, this is termed purchasing power risk. It is the risk that a dollar held today will buy fewer goods tomorrow. Many of your clients have had personal experience with purchasing power risk as they tried to save for tuition, homes and cars. Month by month, they have watched prices jump. Inflation impacts not just savings accounts; it impacts other types of investments and also our clients' insurance programs. For example, high inflation tends to have a negative impact on financial assets, such as bank accounts. Tangible assets, such as real estate and collectibles, tend to rise in value during periods of high inflation.

Inflation can substantially change a client's insurance needs. For example, wage boosts due solely to inflation can cause a client's disability income coverage to become outdated. The amount of life insurance may need to be increased simply to cover the increased dollar figure of liabilities owed or to preserve the survivor's standard of living. Inflation is one reason a periodic review of insurance needs is so important. Even a low rate of inflation can impact a client's needs. For example, even at a three percent inflation level, a client's insurance coverage will be worth one-third less in purchasing power in just a decade.

Default Risk

This involves the loss of principal. It can occur when the organization in which an investment is made goes bankrupt or is otherwise unable to pay off its obligations because of financial strains.

Due to the insolvency crisis of the early 1990s and 2000s, clients became concerned about the default risk involved in taking out an insurance policy. They wonder if the funds will be there when promised. One way to deal with these concerns is to provide your clients with the reports of two or three insurance company credit reporting companies, such as A. M. Best, S&P, Moody's or Duff & Phelps. Even here, one needs to be leery as we learned from the sub-prime mortgage mess, in which some of the ratings companies failed to evaluate the soundness of the investments correctly.

Other Risks

There are other types of investment risk that you may wish to discuss with your clients, depending on their individual situations. These include legislative risk, call risk, and additional commitment risk.

Legislative risk involves the possibility that the law that provides a favorable environment for an investment may change. For example, the 1986 Tax Reform Act cut down the appeal of many highly-leveraged oil and gas tax shelters. Whether the estate tax will be repealed is an important factor. Whether life settlements will lead to the abolishment of the tax advantages of life insurance is a question. Tax laws change continually, and those changes have an impact on investments.

Call risk involves the possibility that a client may invest in a high-yield debt instrument only to have the debtor repay the debt prior to its due date. In other words, the investor gets less interest than initially anticipated. This sometimes happens with corporate bonds in a falling interest rate environment. The debt is usually refinanced at a lower rate and the original investors paid off. *Additional commitment risk* involves the need to put more funds into an investment. In today's environment, you will be involved in a great deal of fact finding that will touch upon broad investment discussions. You will have a familiarity with the type of assets held by your clients and the type of risks typically associated with those assets. On the other side of the ledger, you will have familiarity with the liabilities owed by your clients and the risks they assume along with those debts. You will be asked to help fit the client's insurance program into this context.

Remind clients that:

- Through their day-to-day living patterns, most individuals have assumed an element of risk.
- There is generally a trade-off between risk and reward. The more risk assumed, the greater the expected return. Stated another way, lower returns are associated with lower risk.

RISK TOLERANCE

Your experience has already taught you that some of your clients can accept risk more easily than others.

Defining Risk Tolerance

The degree to which one is willing to accept risk can be defined as one's risk tolerance. You see this every day in property and casualty policies as some clients opt for very low deductibles while others choose very high deductibles. Those who opt for the higher deductibles take the risk of eventual greater out-of-pocket costs at the time of a loss, in return for lower current premiums.

Risk Spectrum

One can make an analogy to a scale when measuring risk. For simplicity's sake, let's assume this risk measurement scale ranges from zero to 100. Some of your clients will stand at zero, others at 100, but most will fall somewhere in between. Those who stand at zero are extremely risk-averse. The closer one moves to 100, the greater degree of risk tolerance. Those who stand at 100 could be viewed not only as completely tolerant of risk but as risk seekers. Those who stand somewhere in between can be considered risk tolerant in various degrees.

Clients need to understand where they stand on the scale. As an advisor, you need to understand both the scale and the fact that different clients have different degrees of risk tolerance. Some recommendations are appropriate for those who are willing to accept risk but inappropriate for those who are risk-averse. Prudent marketplace practice dictates that advisors should assume that most clients are risk-averse. This assumption automatically adds a level of caution to any recommendation.

Assessing risk tolerance often begins with client education. Before clients can fully appreciate the risk involved in any recommendation, they must have some basic knowledge of the different types of investments and the risks associated with them.

Categories of Investments

There are four basic categories of investments that clients should understand so you are able to gauge their risk tolerance. These four investment categories are grouped from lower to higher risk levels as follows:

1. *Cash Equivalents.* These are investments that are highly liquid and have either a non-specified maturity date or a maturity date of less than one year into the future. Short-term certificates of deposit and money market funds are examples. Cash equivalents are considered to be very low-risk investments. Typically, they offer relatively low rates of return.

2. *Longer-Term Debt Instruments.* Large corporations, local jurisdictions and the federal government all issue debt instruments to cover expenses. These debt instruments are typically issued in the form of bonds whose repayment safety is judged by rating agencies such as S&P and Moody's. Their maturity dates are greater than one year. For example, investors typically hold federal government bonds with durations of 5 and 10 years.

   Longer-term debt instruments contain a greater degree of risk than cash equivalents. Default and interest rate risk are the types of risks typically associated with these investments. As a general rule, the longer the term of the debt, the greater the degree of risk. These instruments, for example, are susceptible to a drop in value when inflation rises. Typically, longer-term debt instruments offer higher rates of return when compared to cash equivalents. In effect, there is added payment for the greater degree of risk assumed.

3. *Equity Investments.* Common stock, preferred stock and mutual funds are equity-type investments. They represent ownership in a business. If the business prospers, the value of the stock rises. If the business fails, the stock becomes worthless. As a general rule, in most business cycles, the equity-type investments offer greater opportunity for higher returns than do cash equivalents or debt instruments. Not only do stocks appreciate, but also company profits may be distributed in the form of dividends.

   Clients need to understand that equity-type investments carry substantial risk. Profits don't always increase. The business cycle does not always expand. In a poor business climate, dividends may be stopped as the stock falls in value.

4. *Direct Investments.* Clients sometimes invest their money directly in various business ventures. Typical examples of direct investment are rental real estate or a small business. Direct investments offer various degrees of risk and potential return, depending upon individual circumstances. They typically require far more direct management than do other types of investments. They also offer

the potential for substantial returns but typically carry substantial risk.

For example, clients may be small-business owners. The decision they face is whether or not to reinvest earnings from the business back into the business. If the business flourishes, the returns can far exceed those offered by other opportunities. If the business fails, however, not only will the source of annual income be lost, but excess earnings will be depleted as well. Many owners prefer to lower their risks by placing a portion of their savings in assets unrelated to their business ventures and legally shielded from business liabilities.

Risk Tolerance Assessment Techniques

Given the importance of a client's tolerance toward risk, how does one make an assessment? While there is no one absolute way, we offer three suggested methods to gauge a client's risk tolerance:

- an investment philosophy test
- an examination of investment history
- a review of investment objectives

Investment Philosophy Test

The investment philosophy test aims at uncovering a client's risk tolerance through a series of questions. The test usually takes the form of a questionnaire, with a scoring device that quantifies a client's preference for a conservative, moderate, or aggressive investment strategy.

Examination of Investment History

The past is often considered the prologue to the future. One way to gauge a client's risk tolerance is to examine the type of investments the client made in the past. For example, clients who placed their savings solely in certificates of deposit would, in all likelihood, have a very low level of risk tolerance.

Review of Investment Objectives

Another way of gauging risk tolerance is to ask clients about their financial objectives with follow-up questions designed to uncover the client's feelings about various topics related to risk. These follow-up questions would typically concern safety of principal, tax reduction, and asset appreciation strategies.

Other follow-up questions would probe the client's feelings regarding the need for liquidity, generation of current income, and inflation. The client's answers to both the financial objective(s) and follow-up questions provide the agent with a source of information from which the client's risk-tolerance level can be inferred.

RISK MANAGEMENT

Risk management seeks to balance the risks of an individual's various investment decisions; one against the other. One of the best ways of managing risk is through financial diversification. Risk management through diversification offers an opportunity for the clients with low risk tolerances to balance loss of principal concerns against needs for capital appreciation. Risk management through diversification also offers clients with higher risk tolerance the opportunity to balance growth investments with sources of steady return.

For example, a client might balance a decision to place money in a CD against a decision to purchase an aggressive mutual fund offered by your company. While the fund may soar up and down, the CD provides a steady return. While the savings in the CD risk loss of purchasing power, the amount put into the aggressive fund offers the opportunity to achieve returns substantially above the inflation level.

There are a variety of ways to manage risk through diversification. A client can diversify investment decisions by holding a variety of assets such as stocks, bonds, and real estate. A client can diversify within an asset category. For example, a client can buy several mutual funds with different objectives. A client can also diversify the timing of financial decisions. For example, CDs can be scheduled to mature over a period of years, allowing an adjustment mechanism for varying rates of interest.

The role of risk management through diversification is an important issue for an agent to take into consideration in developing a client's financial plans.

JUDGING THE CLIENT'S SITUATION

No single approach can be effectively used with all clients. Nor will a single solution apply to all clients. Client risk profiles vary, client needs vary, and client objectives vary.

Continuing Service

A recommendation made today may not be valid tomorrow. The financial and personal needs and goals of individuals change over time. For example, a young couple may need mortgage protection at age 30, college accumulation at age 40, and estate planning at age 55. In some instances, your recommendations and the product selection may take these evolving needs into consideration. In other instances, this is not possible. For example, the death of a spouse followed by remarriage can substantially alter a client's needs and goals.

This is why it is important to establish the practice of periodically reviewing a client's needs. In addition, this periodic review helps to cement the relationship between the insurance professional and his or her client. The financial services professional becomes part of an ongoing monitoring of the client's needs and the solutions to those needs. Record keeping becomes an important part of this process. All of us would like to think that each of our clients is special and that we retain the details of their plans in a mental notebook. Operating on such a basis, however, invites confusion and by necessity downplays the very details that often differentiate one client's situation from that of another. Insurance professionals should, therefore, make it a practice to conduct their periodic reviews with the help of fact-finding aids. Detailed notes should be taken and kept with the client's other records. This provides the insurance professional with a clear method of refreshing his or her memory as to the particulars of each client situation.

Practical Aids for Determining Suitability and Finding Facts

We have seen that fact finding and suitability are important. There are aids available to help determine suitability and uncover the appropriate facts.

Organized Fact Finders

Some agents try to uncover information simply through the interview process without the use of any guiding aid. This is not a recommended process in today's ethics-sensitive environment. Simply put, it has too many opportunities for error and provides little documentation. Some needed information may not be acquired and other information may be forgotten. Prudence suggests the use of an organized fact finder.

Most companies make such fact finders available. Some fact finders are relatively simple, others more detailed. The selection of a particular fact finder will depend in part on your comfort level and expertise with the type of questions presented and, in part, on the relative complexity involved in the particular client situation.

Government Tax Form(s) as Fact Finder

In addition to company or commercially developed fact finders, agents may wish to use government forms. For example, reviewing the 1040 income tax return with a client can pinpoint many issues from the possible redirection of tax dollars to the need for greater retirement savings. Agents involved in estate planning may find that the estate tax Form 706 Estate Tax Return is helpful as a source of third-party influence as to the impact of estate taxes, it also requires the assembly of comprehensive information for proper completion.

Dialogue of Key Questions as Fact Finder

Some planners are very comfortable using the typical fill-in-the-figure type fact finders. Other agents are more comfortable using a suggested dialogue of questions designed to elicit pertinent information from the client. Many of these questions are purposefully designed to be disturbing. In other words, they provide a track for an agent to follow that causes the client to stop and think about his or her current situation. Some agents use a combination of both tools.

Multiple Purpose Form

A fact finder serves more than one purpose. The most obvious purpose is the organized guidance it provides an agent in assembling the pertinent information about a client. The nature of a fact finder establishes a professional pattern for the agent. Its use ensures that each client is treated in a similar and proper fashion.

A fact finder also serves as an important reference tool. Initially, the fact finder may be used to sort through information. It is a relatively easy way, for example, to pinpoint information inconsistencies. It's a way to test a new plan to see if the agent's proposal meets the client's needs.

Review Item: Jumping the Gun

Agent Scully: "So, you're a fan of Clint Eastwood and drive a sports car. I have just the product for you."

Is the agent jumping to conclusions about his client's risk-tolerance level? What steps would you suggest to the agent before he makes an inappropriate product recommendation?

The fact finder will eventually serve as a reference for historical information that can be used to conduct periodic reviews. What type of assets did the client own 5 years ago? Has the client's net worth increased or decreased? Have new family members entered into the situation? Have intervening deaths altered the client's initial objectives? In other words, the fact finder serves as a useful reference tool in conducting periodic reviews.

From a compliance standpoint, fact finders can serve as evidence of ethical conduct and appropriate agent recommendations should questions arise at a future date about why an action was taken.

Fact-Finder Format and Compliance Considerations

Some fact finders limit their format to information gathering. Other fact finders provide additional information that can be used to educate the client or stimulate need. Marketplace practice issues may arise, depending on how a fact finder that contains additional information is used during the sales process. If the fact finder is being used solely as part of the interview process, few marketplace practice issues arise. The added information could be considered to be cues and prompts for the agent as he or she conducts the information gathering.

On the other hand, marketplace practice issues can arise if a fact finder that goes beyond mere information gathering is left with a client to complete. For example, a fact finder might contain prohibited language, implying that a comprehensive financial and investment plan would occur as a result of the form completion. The inclusion of such language in a fact finding packet delivered to a client for self-completion would be inappropriate if the agent was not a registered investment advisor (RIA). In addition, under FINRA/NASD compliance rules, agents who are RIAs must be certain that the fact finders used in their practices have been reviewed by their broker-dealer(s) prior to use. If you are unsure as to whether or not you are using an approved form, call your home office for verification. It is far better to err on the side of caution than to open yourself to charges of improper business practices that could result in a ruined reputation.

Supplementary Information

Life underwriters are dealing in an environment where many securities-type standards are being applied. It is also indicated that this should not be an onerous burden for agents. In fact, many of these standards offer agents a road map of protection in instances of legal action, as well as increased sales opportunities brought about through greater client services. Many securities representatives apply business-type financial planning concepts to their client dealings.

With this fact in mind, financial services professionals should seriously consider incorporating simplified financial statements into the fact-finding process. A net worth statement would be typical of this type of information. A cash flow or budget statement may also prove helpful in developing a client's financial profile. In some cases, the client is able to prepare these statements. In other cases, these statements will be prepared through the joint work of the agent and his or her client(s). In still other cases, the client's accountant will supply this information.

Fact Finders
The following are examples of fact finders: • net worth statement—a client's financial history   • annual budget and cash flow statement   • client budget—estimates versus actual dollars

REGULATION OF FINANCIAL PLANNING PROFESSIONALS

Most of this chapter has been devoted to spelling out the obligations of financial services professionals who deal with insurance and related products. If you are engaged as a financial planner, be aware that a broader scope of ethical responsibility is involved, and that there is federal monitoring of your behavior.

Your ethical responsibility is that of a fiduciary acting on behalf of your clients and your services are likely to fall under the jurisdiction of the Securities and Exchange Commission (SEC). Your behavior should be guided by the dictates of the Investment Advisers Act of 1940. This requires you to register as an investment advisor with the SEC and agree to abide by strict standards of ethical conduct. In addition, many states are moving toward stricter regulation of financial planners.

As an investment advisor, you are governed by the FINRA/NASD Rules of Conduct.

FINRA/NASD Rules of Conduct

Under the 1934 act, FINRA/NASD must promulgate rules designed to

- prevent fraudulent practices and promote equitable principles of trade
- safeguard against unreasonable profits, commissions, or other charge
- prevent unfair discrimination between customers, issuers, or broker-dealers
- provide for appropriate discipline for the violation of its rules (for example, censure, suspension and expulsion)

The FINRA/NASD Rules of Conduct require that member broker-dealers and associated persons of broker-dealers observe high standards of commercial honor, as well as just and equitable principles of trade. The rules regulate a wide range of activity relating to such areas as the sale of securities, suitability of such sales, confirmation of transactions and supervision.

The rules of conduct govern (1) the supervision of the salespersons, (2) private securities transactions, (3) outside business activities of associated persons, (4) suitability and fair dealing with customers, (5) influencing or rewarding employees of other broker-dealers and finders fees and (6) sales literature, advertising and communications with the public. Some of these rules are considered in the paragraphs that immediately follow.

1. *Supervision.* A broker-dealer must establish and maintain a system of specified written oversight and review procedures to supervise the activities of each registered representative.
2. *Private Securities Transactions.* This area involves any securities transactions beyond the regular scope of an associated person's relationship with a broker-dealer such as new offerings of

securities, which are not registered with the SEC. Thus, it is incumbent upon the broker-dealer to train and continually remind its registered representatives (including its life insurance agents) that the definition of a security is very broad and any activity even remotely resembling a securities transaction should be brought to the brokers-dealer's attention for approval.

3. *Outside Business Activities of Associated Persons.* Article III, Sec. 43 of the FINRA/NASD Rules prohibits an associated person of a broker-dealer from accepting employment or compensation concerning any business activity outside the scope of the broker-dealer employment relationship unless the person provides the broker-dealer with prompt written notice.

For our purposes, the most important regulation is that of suitability and fair dealing, which we have already mentioned. To reiterate:

4. *Suitability and Fair Dealing with Customers.* Article III, Section 2 of the FINRA/NASD Rules provides that in recommending to a customer the purchase or sale of any security, a member shall have reasonable grounds for believing that the recommendation is suitable for such customer upon the basis of the facts, if any, disclosed by such customer as to his other securities holdings and as to his financial situation and needs.

In recommending a product, a registered representative must have reasonable grounds to believe that the product being recommended is suitable for his or her customer. Such determination should be based on customer disclosures as to income, net worth, securities holdings, life insurance, real estate holdings, customer financial sophistication, investment objectives and financial needs. Registered principals of the broker-dealer make the final determination as to suitability and the acceptance of the transaction.

In a variation on the suitability theme, the SEC recognizes a broker-dealer obligation of fair dealing under the general antifraud provisions of the federal securities laws. The commission maintains that a violation of the suitability doctrine may constitute a violation of Rule 10b-5 under the Securities Exchange Act of 1934, which is the SEC's general antifraud rule under the act. This position is predicated on the theory that when a broker-dealer holds itself out as a broker-dealer (solicits business), it implicitly represents that it will recommend securities only when it has a reasonable basis that such are suited to the customer's needs.

Judicial decisions have contributed to the development of suitability as a fraud concept outside the antifraud provisions of the federal securities laws. In *Anderson v. Knox*, for example, a federal Court of Appeals held that an insurance agent who had induced a client to buy excessive amounts of bank-financed insurance was liable for damages for common law fraud since the policies were unsuitable for the policyowner's needs. Judicial thinking, scholarly works and regulatory attitudes suggest that criminal and civil liabilities attendant to the suitability and fair-dealing concepts set forth in the FINRA/NASD rules have yet to reach their full potential.

Sales Literature, Advertising, and Communications with the Public. A series of SEC and FINRA/NASD rules and guidelines has evolved to govern advertising, sales literature, and communications with the public concerning the distribution of equity products.

Communications with the Public. Article III, Sec. 35 of the FINRA/NASD Rules of Conduct mandates that every item of advertising and sales literature (the definition of which is quite broad) be approved by a registered principal of the broker-dealer prior to its use. Furthermore, such material must contain a broker-dealer's name, the identity of the preparer of the material, and the date first published. Advertisements and sales literature must also be filed with FINRA/NASD within 10 days of their first use. Such materials can be disapproved for failure to meet FINRA/NASD guidelines.

On the Insurance Side—FINRA/NASD has established a Variable Life Insurance Marketing Guide. Prior to 1990, FINRA/NASD policy emphasized that the primary attribute of a variable life insurance (VLI) policy is its death benefit, even though VLI also contains an important investment aspect in its cash value. FINRA/NASD opined, however, that VLI should not be described as an investment. With the advent of single-premium VLI policies, the FINRA/NASD revised its position to permit broker-dealers to give more weight to the investment element of policies or contracts. By 1990, FINRA/NASD further relaxed its position and moved to imposing no absolute requirement that broker-dealers maintain a "balance" in describing the insurance and investment elements of a VLI policy. However, communications should describe both elements.

By early 1994, the FINRA/NASD/ had in place SEC-approved guidelines covering variable products to govern the preparation of and communication with the public through advertising and sales literature. The primary thrust of such guidelines is to prohibit referring to variable products as mutual funds. The guidelines require that communications concerning variable products clearly identify the product as either a variable life insurance policy or a variable annuity contract; avoid implying that the underlying product is a mutual fund (since there are significant differences between mutual funds and variable contracts); avoid presenting variable products as short-term liquid investments; disclose the impact of early withdrawal such as sales loads, tax penalties and potential loss of principal in references to liquidity; and avoid suggestion that guarantees apply to investment returns. In addition, by mid-1994, the SEC approved a new set of FINRA/NASD/NASD guidelines limiting the use of rankings by mutual funds and other investment companies (including separate accounts underlying variable insurance products) in advertising and marketing materials.

With respect to illustrations, the methodology and format of hypothetical illustrations must be patterned after the required illustrations used in the variable life insurance prospectus approved by the SEC. Illustrations must reflect the maximum guaranteed mortality and expense charges associated with the policy for each assumed rate of return. Current charges may also be illustrated in addition to the maximum charges. An illustration may utilize any combination of investment returns, up to and including a gross rate of 12 percent, if one of the returns illustrated is a 0 percent gross rate. However, even though the maximum rate of 12 percent may be acceptable, FINRA/NASD does require that the broker-dealer confirm that such maximum rate illustrated is reasonable in light of market conditions and available investment options. Mandating the illustration of a 0 percent rate of return demonstrates how the absence of growth in the underlying investment account can affect policy values and reinforces the hypothetical nature of the illustration. FINRA/NASD guidelines also permit comparisons between variable life insurance contracts and other financial instruments based on actual experience, not assumed hypothetical performance. Performance comparisons must be fair, balanced and complete and must comply with FINRA/NASD rules governing communications with the public. In addition, the SEC has imposed performance-comparison advertising rules, including standardized computation of performance data in advertising and sales literature for mutual funds and variable annuities.

As indicated previously, the format of any personalized variable life insurance illustration must be filed with and its use must be approved in advance by the Advertising Department of FINRA/NASD. The sale of variable life insurance and the use of personalized illustrations can be conducted only by salespersons registered with FINRA/NASD. FINRA/NASD rules mandate that each broker-dealer review, supervise and store all sales materials including illustrations.

CHAPTER REVIEW QUESTIONS

Answers to Review Questions are in the Appendix.

1. After agent Smith has conducted a thorough fact finding with client Jones, agent Smith should
   - (A) retain these records for use in future periodic reviews
   - (B) discard these records as quickly as possible to eradicate all documentation of the sales process
   - (C) archive the records for 6 months before destroying
   - (D) forward all records to the client for documentation

2. The FINRA/NASD Conduct Rules
   - (A) constitute an undue and illegal hardship on financial advisors selling variable products
   - (B) emphasize the need to provide proper client service, including disclosure of confidential information regarding your company's investment philosophy and trading positions
   - (C) are statutorily inapplicable to insurance agents
   - (D) emphasize the need to provide proper client service, including efforts made to understand a client's current financial condition

3. Which of the following statements is true concerning model legislation promulgated by the National Association of Insurance Commissioners (NAIC)?

    (A) NAIC model legislation applies only to agents, not to home offices.
    (B) NAIC model legislation is designed to cover only home office marketing practices.
    (C) NAIC model legislation is designed for implementation by the federal government.
    (D) NAIC model legislation gives state insurance commissioners substantial powers to investigate both carriers and agents suspected of violating the law.

4. Which of the following is an example of an equity investment?

    (A) a federal government bond with a 30-year duration
    (B) a short-term certificate of deposit
    (C) a local jurisdiction bond with a 5-year duration
    (D) common stock

5. Which of the following statements regarding risk tolerance is true?

    (A) All clients maintain the same level of risk tolerance.
    (B) Some clients can accept risk more easily than others.
    (C) Risk tolerance is inapplicable to an agent's insurance practice.
    (D) Risk tolerance is applicable to property and casualty and inapplicable to an agent's life insurance practice.

6. Agents should assume that most clients are

    (A) risk-averse
    (B) risk seekers
    (C) tolerant of moderate levels of risk
    (D) tolerant of high levels of risk

7. Legislative risk involves

    (A) the possibility that the law, which currently provides a favorable environment for an investment, may change
    (B) the possibility that the law, which currently provides a hostile environment for an investment, may change
    (C) exposure to investment default
    (D) exposure to investment appreciation

8.   A client's risk tolerance will

   (A)   remain static over time
   (B)   typically evolve over time
   (C)   be generally lowered due to media and cultural influences
   (D)   be generally unaffected by media and cultural influences

READ THE FOLLOWING DIRECTIONS BEFORE CONTINUING

The questions below differ from the preceding questions in that they all contain the word EXCEPT. So you understand fully the basis used in selecting each answer, be sure to read each question carefully.

9.   All of the following are suggested methods of assessing a client's tolerance towards risk EXCEPT

   (A)   the investment philosophy test
   (B)   the 80/20 analysis
   (C)   the examination of investment history
   (D)   the review of investment objectives

10.   All of the following are major categories of investment risk EXCEPT

   (A)   purchasing power risk
   (B)   market risk
   (C)   default risk
   (D)   fluctuation risk

Learning Objectives

An understanding of the material in this chapter should enable the student to

1. List the steps involved in the ethical sales process.

2. Describe misrepresentation and false advertising as ethical missteps within the sales process.

3. Explain the principles and benefits of full disclosure.

4. List and describe the four keys to full disclosure.

ETHICAL SALES

The Sales Presentation

In this chapter, we will cover a variety of marketing practices that financial services professionals (particularly those engaged in selling insurance) should avoid, including false advertising, misrepresentation and lack of full disclosure.

After determining the needs of the client and the suitability of the planning strategies, you come to a point where you need to recommend or sell a product. In that case, you are involved in a sales presentation. Let's define a sales presentation as that part of the process that follows an agent's fact finding and determination of client objectives. A sales presentation occurs when an agent presents recommendations designed to solve a client's needs and objectives. The presentation can be thought of as a five-part process; the first two steps take place before the actual presentation.

- The agent reviews the data obtained and considers various solutions based on his or her expertise and experience that might solve the client's needs and objectives. This might involve consideration of just one solution, but far more likely three or four of them.

- The agent selects one or two recommendations that best serve the client's needs.
- The agent meets with his or her client and makes the recommendation(s).
- The agent explains to the client the reasons behind the recommendation(s).
- The agent uses his or her sales skills to bring closure by having the client take action on the recommendation(s).

Review Item: Making a Presentation
Agent Smith: "Your policy has guaranteed and nonguaranteed elements. . . ."
Client Jones (thinking): He's been talking for half an hour. If only he'd show me how this policy works!
How should the agent present the information to the client? What is the client's likely learning style?

Six Necessary Steps in an Ethically Sound Sales Process

In this section, we outline what is required for an ethically sound sales process.

1. *Gain Client Attention*

   Before you start to discuss a product with a client, make sure you gain his or her attention and convey the importance of the information that you are about to relay. Sometimes, a client appears to be disinterested. He or she may say that your advice is trustworthy and no further explanation is required. This may be flattering, but it is potentially dangerous to your relationship with the client.

   We suggest that you handle such a situation by telling the client that part of your job is to make sure he or she understands what is being proposed. Keep in mind that if there are any future misunderstandings or dissatisfactions with the product, the client or the potential beneficiaries are unlikely to remember their initial disinterest. The responsibility will rest on your shoulders. Document your efforts through a follow-up letter outlining the proposal and explanation.

2. *Explain Policy Structure*

Educate your client on the structure of a life insurance policy and how it works. An illustration can help you do this by demonstrating the three key components that your client must understand; namely, the premium, the cash value and the death benefit. The properly constructed illustration will also help you explain the difference between guaranteed and non-guaranteed cash values and death benefits.

3. *Illustrate Downside Risk*

   You should seriously consider the use of more than one illustration to show the downside risk in policy performance. This will help to demonstrate how the recommended policy is expected to perform under various market conditions. It will also help to set realistic performance expectations in the client's mind.

4. *Clarify Coverage Components*

   Sometimes, a portion of the insurance coverage is provided by term riders, paid for with dividends or excess interest. Dividends and excess interest are not guaranteed elements of a life insurance policy. They change over time as a company's actual experience varies from its original assumptions. Often, clients do not understand this. Be sure your clients are not among this group. Fully explain what portion is term and what portion is permanent coverage and how each portion is being funded. Do not let your client be under the assumption that his or her blended policy is just another name for traditional permanent coverage with all its guarantees.

5. *Explain Who Bears What Risk*

   Nearly all insurance coverage sold today contains both a level of guaranteed performance as well as enhancements beyond those guarantees. This dual performance system of minimum guarantees, combined with potential enhancement, is unique to the life insurance product. This is one reason why it is so difficult for many consumers to understand this product. As part of the illustration disclosure process, educate your client on the risks involved. In other words, point out that the insurance company bears the risk on the guaranteed elements in the policy, while the client bears the risks on the non-guaranteed elements.

6. *Comply with Regulations and Mandated Standards*

Most companies now provide their financial advisors and brokers with guidelines regarding the illustrations that will be provided to clients. These guidelines have been drafted for the protection of the client, the company and you. Failure to follow them puts your career at risk and could create unrealistic expectations on the part of the client which could leave the carrier open to lawsuits, impeding its ability to operate on a competitive basis. In addition, failure to follow these guidelines can mean limitations in your E&O coverage and can also weaken your legal position should client complaints arise at a future date.

Client Education

Information may not be enough. The client may not comprehend what you are saying without knowledge of how financial products work and, thus, may need to be educated. How do you know whether or not a client needs to be educated? Ask the client questions. The answers to your questions will indicate whether or not more explanation is necessary. The answers will also provide an indication of whether or not the client is misinterpreting what you are saying.

Client Education Is Selling

Client education is not just teaching. Client education is selling. If a client does not understand what you are saying, the chances are that he or she will not understand why he or she should buy your product(s). The client simply won't comprehend the need. Client education and quizzing will provide you with feedback. If a client initially doesn't understand something, you'll know and have an opportunity to present the same concept in a different way.

Client Learning Styles

Keep in mind that some of us learn better by hearing, some by seeing, others by quietly sitting and reading. A one-page chart, for example, might be the best way to convey the need for a funded buy-sell agreement to a visual learner. The second business partner may learn best by hearing. In that case, a lecture type presentation might be the best way to convey basically the same information. A written proposal might work best for a third, reading-oriented partner.

Tools for Educating Clients

Professionals engaged in selling life insurance should be aware of two excellent sources that can be used to educate clients in the basics of life insurance: the *Life Insurance Buyer's Guide* and *What You Should Know about Buying Life Insurance*. The *Life Insurance Buyer's Guide* contains a concise explanation of life insurance products. Many states have regulations that require that the guide be provided, along with a policy summary to prospective life insurance consumers. The guide is an excellent way to educate your clients and help them understand the different insurance options available to them. This knowledge makes them active participants in the buying process. Many companies have tailored versions of the *Life Insurance Buyer's Guide* for distribution to clients.

What You Should Know about Buying Life Insurance has been developed by the American Council of Life Insurance (ACLI). It provides readers with basics about life insurance in addition to information about choosing an agent and purchasing insurance. *What You Should Know about Buying Life Insurance* has been endorsed by the National Association of Insurance and Financial Advisors (NAIFA) and the Life and Health Insurance Foundation for Education (LIFE). The booklet serves as an excellent third-party influence piece that will support other information you provide to your clients.

ETHICAL MISSTEPS

Up to this point we have covered the rules of fair practice and outlined what a proper approach to presenting and selling products would involve. Throughout these processes, the professional must avoid two missteps: misrepresentation and/or false advertising. We examine these two issues below.

Misrepresentation

Misrepresentation is defined as "an untrue statement, whether unintentional or deliberate. It may be a form of nondisclosure where there is a duty to disclose, or the planned creation of a false appearance." This definition indicates that misrepresentation has the following three characteristics.

1. The speaker provided a statement that must be relied upon by the victim and this reliance must be justified.
2. The speaker must know that the victim is relying on the factual correctness of his or her statements.

3. The misrepresentation needs to have resulted in a loss to the victim.

Misrepresentation can occur as a result of agents's desire to deceive or through negligence. Negligence is defined as a "lack of care or failure to do what is reasonable and prudent in the circumstances." Professionals are negligent when they lack knowledge they should possess by virtue of their position as an expert. This negligence is both morally and legally wrong because it is a failure of the professional requirement of diligence.

Misrepresentation can also be deliberate, although it usually concerns the deliberate omission of important information rather than an overt act of deception. An example is when a practitioner fails to mention the drawbacks of a particular financial product (such as high surrender charges) or the possible negative consequences of a purchase (possible difficulty in obtaining additional life insurance if a client has participated in an Investor-Owned Life Insurance transaction). In these cases, misrepresentation is similar to fraud, since they are both forms of lying.

Lying is a deliberate (intentional) attempt to convince someone to believe something that the speaker knows is not true. People can lie through failing to provide information that is material to the matter at hand, they can lie through both words and gestures and they can lie by communicating outright untruths as if they were facts. Whichever form a lie takes, the intention of the speaker is the same in each case. The speaker seeks to persuade the listener to act in ways that he or she would not act if all of the relevant information was available. For example, you know that you would never have bought that "lemon" of a used car if you knew that it was totaled out after a recent hurricane. If you would have known that information (which all rational persons would agree is materially relevant), you would have acted differently. Of course, this is precisely what the used car salesperson feared and why he or she did not tell you about it in the first place.

It is the sense of unfairness provoked by the example above that provides a clue as to what is wrong with lying. Lying is wrong since the speaker undermines the victim's ability to make a sound decision in his or her own best interest. In the example, the used car salesperson took away the victim's choice and used the victim as a means to achieve the salesperson's own ends, selling the "lemon" and getting a good price for it. Using another person in this way violates the Golden Rule (a foundational principle in all religious traditions) which commands us to treat other people as we would like to be treated. Although there are often prudential reasons for not lying, such as the financial benefits of a reputation for honest dealing, the primary moral reason concerns what other people deserve from us on account of their dignity and autonomy. Since lying is unjust, immoral and exploitative, it is wrong and, since misrepresentation and fraud are forms of lying, they must be avoided as well.

However, the line between vigorously trying to sell a product and misrepresentation can be difficult to determine. From an ethical point of view, disclosure is a complicated issue for the financial services professional who sells products. The question becomes, "How much is the financial services professional ethically obliged to disclose?" It is an accepted principle of effective salesmanship (not to be confused with ethical salesmanship) not to say anything negative about the product and certainly not to disclose shortcomings unnecessarily. For example, if you are selling your home, is it necessary to point out all of the defects that only you know? If you do, you probably will succeed in discouraging every prospect from buying it. But this analogy is not quite right, since the exchange that occurs between the buyer and seller of a home is not the same as the exchange between a financial services professional and his or her client. The financial services professional is bound to look out for the interests of the client in a way that the home owner is not. Moreover, the home buyer understands this and is ready to act as his or her own advocate in this transaction. Clients have engaged a professional to use his or her expertise to advance their best interests and, therefore, the financial services professional is held to a higher standard than *caveat emptor*.

False Advertising

Another area of marketing in which a misstep can occur is advertising. Insurance professionals and other financial services professionals must make sure that the materials they use to advertise, sell their products and portray themselves are true and clearly comprehensible. Advertising that contains untrue, unclear, incomplete or deceptive statements is unethical. Furthermore, state laws often specifically prohibit such advertising. The application of these laws not only applies to home office material but also to agency-prepared material or material created by the financial advisor.

Insurance departments are particularly concerned about advertisements that confuse life insurance with a savings plan or investment. Calling premiums "deposits" is unacceptable. Referring to life insurance as a "tax shelter" also invites regulator criticism. As a matter of fact, most codes of ethics suggest that to sell life insurance primarily as a tax shelter is wrong if it has little other benefit as insurance.

For example, when you are using advertising literature in the sales process, be sure it emphasizes the death benefit protection offered by life insurance. While the savings element of life insurance can be an important factor, it is essential that the protection element of life insurance is discussed.

If you prepare customized materials for your clients, recognize that these materials are subject to regulatory oversight. Many companies and home offices have established special units to review these materials. They realize that many creative ideas come from the field, and they are willing to help you satisfy state codes and regulations. Be sure not to bypass the process.

The following are some additional pointers regarding advertising:

- *Testimonials*. Don't use your imagination. Testimonials must be true. Approach satisfied clients about providing you with statements.

- *Insurance*. Don't hide the product you are selling. If you are selling life insurance, this must be clearly stated and not just implied.

- *Statistics*. Don't make up numbers. Base your presentation on facts.

- *Products*. Don't bait and switch. That is, be prepared to sell the product described in your advertising pieces. If you have stressed the economical nature of term, be ready to sell it. Don't retract the letter that opened the door.

- *Type Size*. Don't try to hide the facts in small type. This invites both regulatory and client suspicion. If something is important, say it clearly.

- *Exceptions*. Don't forget the exceptions. If there are exceptions to a policy's coverage, let the client know this in advance. To do otherwise is to invite ethical troubles. Your client may be the very person to whom the exception applies at a critical time.

- *Title*. Don't use a title to indicate that you are something you are not. If you advertise yourself as a financial planner, act accordingly. Remember, financial planners are usually compensated on a fee structure. They must comply with additional levels of regulations and licensing requirements. If you do not intend to do anything but sell insurance, make sure it is reflected on your card.

One final point about false advertising. Be honest and straightforward in presenting yourself and your credentials. Don't portray yourself as an investment advisor if you are not. Don't portray yourself as an expert in fields where you have no expertise. In short, fit the products to the clients' needs, educate the clients and convince them that these products fit those needs. If they don't, you are wrong to try to sell the products.

FULL DISCLOSURE

One of the most important ethical obligations of a financial services professional before and during a sales presentation is full disclosure. Full disclosure means presenting the facts about a product accurately and thoroughly, so that a client can make a valid informed purchase decision.

This is a particular problem for insurance agents because they have not only an ethical obligation, but also a legal obligation to their clients due in great part to the nature of an insurance contract. Unlike other contracts, a life insurance contract is not negotiated. It is a *contract of adhesion*. This means that a life insurance contract is drawn up by one of the parties (the insurer) and either accepted or rejected by the other party (the policyowner).

Because the insurer draws up the contract, the courts have ruled that the insurer bears the burden of making things clear to the policyowner. Because the agent represents the insurance company to the policyowner, he or she must educate the client.

From an ethical point of view, disclosure is a complicated issue for the financial services professional who sells products. How much is the agent ethically obliged to disclose? It is an accepted principle in effective salesmanship (not to be confused with ethical salesmanship) not to say anything negative about the product one is selling and certainly not to disclose shortcomings unnecessarily. So two questions arise: How much does one need to disclose, and to what extent can failure to disclose be construed as market misconduct? To answer those questions, reflect for a moment on two points: first, reflect on how selling is a market transaction, and second, reflect on how lack of disclosure is similar to lying.

Selling insurance and other financial products is, among other things, a market transaction. In the ideal market transaction, two people decide to exchange goods because they hope the exchange will benefit both of them. That is the genius of the free market system. Freedom of exchange leads to the overall improvement of the traders' lot. In a market exchange, nothing new has been produced, but both people are better off because of the trade.

Ideally, there is perfect information about the worth of what is being given and received in return. Such a trade, freely entered into with full information, should maximize satisfaction on both sides.

However, if one of the parties is misled into believing a product is not what it is because it is misrepresented, the effect of both sides being better off and satisfied is undermined. Deception leads to the deceived party getting something different and less valuable than what is expected. The deceived party most likely would not have entered into the exchange had he or she known the full truth about the product. The conditions for an ideal trade include the freedom or autonomy of the participants and full knowledge of the pertinent details of the product, both of which are required if we are to have what is often called informed consent. Consent cannot be presumed to be given if one is either forced into an exchange or lacks adequate knowledge of the product one is bargaining for. A choice based on inadequate information is not a choice at all.

We talked earlier about misrepresentation being a lie. Is failure to disclose also a lie? Some would say, "Not disclosing isn't lying, it's just not telling." But that misses the point. Deliberately withholding information to get another to act contrary to the way he or she would have acted with the information has the same deceptive structure and consequence as the overt lie. It doesn't allow an informed choice.

Still another question occurs: Must one disclose everything? Certainly some failure to disclose is wrong, but how much must we disclose? The characterization of lying we gave above should help us decide. Whenever you are tempted not to disclose something, ask yourself why you are not disclosing. Withholding information because you fear losing the sale if the consumer or client knows the whole story is manipulating. You might object, saying there are times when one does not benefit from not disclosing, such as on social occasions. For example, when your friend asks how you are, you don't have to disclose that you feel miserable. Your friend probably doesn't want to hear it. Or when your friend asks how he looks, you don't have to say, "Like you just got out of bed." That kind of social nondisclosure is acceptable because in those cases, one is not trying to change the behavior of another to personally benefit from it. Hence, if one lies for a reason other than manipulating the behavior of the one being lied to, that kind of lie may not be wrong. Having said that though, we should introduce a caveat: In such social situations, there may be a great deal of paternalism involved, and a great many assumptions being made about what the other wants or needs. It is not clear that it is a totally harmless activity.

It is the case that, in some situations, it might be hard to decide how much to disclose. Let's consider a brief scenario.

Case Study*

A Trip to Aruba

Brock Roberts, CLU and Cosmic Life agent, needs one more sale to qualify for membership in Cosmic Life's top production club and win a trip to Aruba. Marie, a client who buys all of her insurance from Brock, has a clearly established need for additional insurance. She asks Brock for three proposals from companies with equal credit ratings. Brock presents illustrations from Cosmic Life, Stable Life, and Exciting Life. He accurately demonstrates that all three policies will fill Marie's need. If she chooses Cosmic, Brock will win the trip. Exciting Life pays a first-year commission that is much higher than that paid by the other two carriers, and of the three companies Stable Life has the strongest long-term financial performance history. These facts are unknown to the client. Marie asks Brock to recommend the best of the three. Brock recommends Cosmic to Marie and that is what she buys.

Marie has no inkling that Brock is on the verge of winning a trip to Aruba. Should she know this? Why or why not?

* This case originally appeared in the July 1991 "Strictly Speaking" column by Burke A. Christensen, *Journal of the American Society of CLU & ChFC*; © 1991 The Society of Financial Service Professionals.

As you can imagine, sometimes there is vehement disagreement about whether Brock should disclose the trip. Some say that, even if Brock thinks Cosmic is as good a buy as Stable or Exciting, and even if he feels comfortable recommending it, he should disclose the information about the trip. There are others who will disagree and argue that he need not disclose it.

In discussion of this case, any number of reasons are given for not disclosing. "No one does it." "It's not necessary." "The client trusts me." "Clients don't need all that information, they'll just get confused." "It's no business of the client's." Are these reasonable defenses of the behavior, or are they rationalizations? How is one to decide? In the face of such disagreement, we would suggest adopting the following method: Ask yourself why you would be reluctant to disclose the trip.

If you are reluctant because you think telling the client about the trip will affect the sale, shouldn't you disclose it to give the client that option? If you are reluctant because you think telling the client won't affect the sale because the client trusts you implicitly to do the best for her, then why be reluctant to disclose? If you are reluctant because you think too much disclosure gives too much information and will confuse the client, aren't you putting yourself in the position of deciding how much information the client can handle? How do you determine how much information that is? In withholding possibly relevant information, aren't you creating a questionable paternalistic relationship? Why not just give the client the information and let her decide? As an added consideration, contemplate what would happen if the client buys Cosmic Life on Brock's recommendation and it doesn't perform as well as Stable or Exciting. Later, Marie finds out the sale of Cosmic was tied to an all-expense-paid vacation. How will that look? Admittedly, bad consequences to oneself do not constitute the primary reason to disclose, but they do provide a consideration to keep in mind.

Let's sum up the method that tests when disclosure is necessary. If you are reluctant to tell the client you are selling insurance, ask yourself why. Perhaps you don't think an insurance policy best fits the needs of the client. In that case, you should disclose because you are putting your interest before the best interest of the client. Perhaps you think the client doesn't want insurance so much as a straightforward mutual fund program. In that case, you should disclose, again for the same reason. Are you glossing over the nonguaranteed aspect of cash value projections in variable products? Why? Perhaps you think that if the client realizes the growth promises are not guaranteed, he or she will look for another product. Once again, if that is so, it seems clear you are putting your interests above those of the client and using the client to further your own goals. That violates the central ethical tenet of "Do unto others what you would have done unto you." Such nondisclosure fails to respect the other and treats him or her merely as a means or instrument to be used for your own gratification.

However we resolve the issue now, the question of how much disclosure is necessary in order to avoid manipulation of a client, and whether commissions and other costs should be disclosed, is being talked about and will continue to be talked about intensely for the next few years. Consumers will demand to know what they are buying and financial advisors will be pressured into disclosing more and more. Old practices will be reviewed and reformed. That's how ethics usually solves these issues. For now, the safest and most ethical road is the following: ***When in doubt, disclose!***

Benefit(s) of Full Disclosure

Aside from being the right thing to do, full disclosure helps to avoid legal problems, particularly when a financial advisor has taken the time to maintain records documenting the disclosure. For example, a financial advisor might retain a copy of a letter explaining his or her recommendation to a client, together with a signed copy of the illustration used in the sales presentation.

Keys to Full Disclosure

Full disclosure involves providing your client with four key pieces of information. Typically, this information is provided during the presentation portion of the sales process.

1. **Provide your client with information about the product.**

   Tell the client exactly what the product will and will not do for the client.

2. **Provide your client with information about the company that is offering the product.**

   Make the client aware of the company's history and ratings. Many home offices will readily supply you with this information for distribution to your clients. Provide your client with information about the type of product being purchased. The difference between whole life and term may seem obvious to you, but to many clients this is new information. Don't overlook the basics.

3. **Provide your clients with information about the illustration used in your sales presentation.**

   Be sure to review the difference between guaranteed and nonguaranteed values.

4. **Provide your client with information as to the role of the insurance application.**

   Explain how it's used in the underwriting process and the importance of providing the company with accurate information. If you feel it is appropriate, point out to the client that supplying inaccurate information may ease the individual underwriting process, but may later result in the denial of a claim.

However, beyond the avoidance of legal difficulties, full disclosure enables clients to anticipate how the products they bought will perform. For example, if the client purchases term insurance, he or she will not be surprised when premiums rise. If a client has purchased universal life, the client will know what to expect as interest rates vary from year to year. Full disclosure provides the client, in effect, with ownership of, and participation in, the buying decision. Unpleasant surprises are avoided, policies are retained and referrals are made. Full disclosure helps to create a sense of trust and cements sales by generating client satisfaction.

Remember to provide clients with information about their options. If more than one product will fulfill their current needs, you should tell them. Additionally, you should inform clients about both the short-term and long-term aspects of each of the presented options. For example, you might explain to a 40-year-old that a term policy is cheaper today but, in the long run, is likely to prove more expensive than a permanent policy.

Review Item: Retirement Specialist

Client Stephanie Dunn: "I thought you specialized in retirement planning. That's what your card says. Why are we still discussing life insurance? You haven't even mentioned IRAs."

Agent Loretta Vincent: "I do specialize in retirement planning, but with life insurance."

Does it appear that Agent Vincent has confused the client about her role and the nature of the product she sells? If so, does this raise an ethical issue?

Documenting Full Disclosure

We've already mentioned that full disclosure enhances client satisfaction and lessens the chance of legal liability. We now need to point out the importance of documenting full disclosure. Why is documentation so important? The answer rests in the fact that when problems arise, they often occur many years after the sale. For example, litigation may occur following the death of a client. Questions may arise about the amount of insurance purchased. Heirs may squabble over the selection of the beneficiary designation. A wife may complain about the continued payment of premiums for a disabled husband, asserting that a disability premium waiver was surely chosen.

In other words, you may not be dealing with a satisfied client, but with an irate heir or third-party executor of an estate. In these instances, you no longer have the word of a satisfied client to support you. You are dependent on your recollection and the records that you have maintained.

In other cases, the client may choose to forget what was said at the time of a sale. The uninsurable client may forget that an additional term rider was suggested and rejected at the time an underlying policy was purchased. Once again, you are dependent on your recollection and the records that you have maintained. If a legal action ensues, your contemporaneous written records will be an important part of your defense. (In other words, write down what is happening in your practice now—it may serve a useful compliance purpose later.) In fact, the existence of such records may discourage unfounded lawsuits from even beginning. Remember, even unfounded lawsuits cost you time and money.

Review Item
<div align="center">**Office Sweep**</div>
Agent Daniels: "These files need to be cleaned out. I wonder how long I should keep these papers about last year's sales."
What should this agent do?

Document Your Disclosure Statements

You not only need to disclose, you also need to document your work. Financial services professionals should use disclosure statements for any aspect of a sale that they believe is best explained and documented.

For example, some clients may insist on buying insufficient coverage. In this case, you may wish to document the fact that additional coverage was discussed with the client. Asking the client to sign a compliance-approved statement to that effect provides you with evidence of the thoroughness of your work. Asking the client to sign such a statement may also encourage the client to obtain the needed coverage.

What to Document

You should document three elements of every sale—namely, the reason for the product recommendation, the illustration used as basis of the sale and a disclosure statement.

- *The Reason for the Product Recommendation.* Your records should provide a written trail of the reasons why a particular product was recommended. This will involve retention of records showing that you performed adequate fact finding on which to base the recommended product choice. These records will also show that you took into consideration the client's needs as well as his or her ability to pay the premiums to support the recommended product. If a variable product is being sold, we recommend that records be maintained that provide evidence of the client's risk tolerance.

- *The Illustration Used As Basis of Sale*. We recommend that you prepare three copies of the illustration used to close a sale. Have the client sign both copies and be sure to retain one in your records. (Illustrations are discussed in the next section.)

- *A Disclosure Statement*. Prepare a separate disclosure statement reviewing the type of policy being purchased and how it functions. Review its features, benefits, and costs. Provide a brief explanation of how the policy will meet the client's needs. Have the client sign off on the disclosure statement, and be sure to retain a signed copy for your records.

In the case of insurance, a state insurance department may already have rules regarding what to furnish and retain. Your state may have adopted the Life Insurance Illustrations Model Regulation drafted by the National Association of Insurance Commissioners (NAIC). Among other aspects, the model regulation seeks to protect consumers by establishing stringent guidelines for the illustration of insurance policy elements that are not guaranteed. The disclosure statement should also make reference to the illustration and the fact that both its guaranteed and nonguaranteed elements have been reviewed with the client. The disclosure statement should also verify that the difference between guaranteed and nonguaranteed elements has been explained by the financial advisor and is understood by the client.

How long should you keep these disclosure records? Your state insurance departments have rules regarding retention. We suggest that you keep your records in accordance with the rules of the state in which you do your business.

Disclosure in the Application

One more area that can be a source of confusion is the insurance application itself. Some clients are reluctant to share information with others, whether it be their banker or broker. They have particular difficulty in understanding why financial services professionals need to know so much. This is where your skills as a professional come to bear. The client must understand the importance of providing accurate information on the insurance application so proper underwriting can take place and, likewise, must understand the serious consequences of providing inaccurate information.

Financial services professionals must keep in mind their obligation for full disclosure not only to the client, but also to the carrier. It is their job to bring about an open exchange of complete and accurate information so that the client and the company can reach valid decisions about accepting or declining an insurance risk.

Postsale Disclosure

The need for disclosure does not end with the closing of the sale and the delivery of the insurance policy. Good ethics and good business practice dictate that financial advisors maintain contact with their clients until policies mature or are terminated. Annual reviews and updates keep policyowners informed of both contract performance and their insurance needs. This makes active decision makers of your clients and can help to avoid difficulties when economic and market conditions change.

For example, if policyowners understand how to read and use annual policy statements, they will understand the impact of higher or lower interest rates on the performance of universal life plans. Similarly, if clients have purchased variable policies, they will understand the impact of rising or falling stock market values on policy performance.

Educating policyowners and revisiting policies on a periodic basis plants the seeds for future business. Policyowners will anticipate the possibility of a need for additional coverage. They will view you as a true professional advisor and will feel comfortable about providing your name to friends and associates seeking insurance.

Postsale disclosure also serves to reduce your legal risks. Clients view you as a professional, not a mere representative of deep pockets to be tapped at the first sign of any trouble. In summary, postsale disclosure facilitates the development of clients, future repeat business, referred leads, and reduced legal liability.

Full disclosure means honesty and leads to informed consent. Misrepresentation and false advertising lead a client to make a decision that might not be made if a more honest picture of the product being considered is presented.

CHAPTER REVIEW QUESTIONS

Answers to Review Questions are in the Appendix.

1.   Which of the following is a benefit of full disclosure?

   (A)   It provides unlimited avoidance of potential legal problems.
   (B)   It includes state-mandated bonus commission structures.
   (C)   It results in a waiver of state licensing fees.
   (D)   It limits legal liability and cements sales.

2.   Client education is

   (A)   a function of the home office underwriting department
   (B)   a function of the agency manager
   (C)   limited to teaching
   (D)   part of the sales function

3.   State insurance department "false advertising" laws typically apply to

   (A)   home office-prepared materials but exempt agency- and agent-prepared materials
   (B)   home office- and company-prepared materials, but exempt agent-prepared materials
   (C)   home-office, agency- and agent-prepared materials
   (D)   agency- and agent-prepared materials, but exempt home office-prepared materials

4.   The obligation that an insurance professional must convey accurate information to a client applies

   (A)   only to written information supplied to a client
   (B)   only to oral statements made as part of a sales presentation to a client
   (C)   both to oral statements and written information, intentionally or unintentionally made or supplied to a client
   (D)   both to oral statements and written information, intentionally made or supplied to a client

5.   The two ethical missteps referred to in chapter 7 of the text are

   (A)   replacement and rebating
   (B)   failure to fully disclose information and lying
   (C)   misrepresentation and false advertising
   (D)   forgery and fraud

6.   The text states that an insurance professional's full disclosure duties will

(A)   not include providing full and accurate application information to the carrier

(B)   be limited to providing the applicant with an Insurance Buyer's Guide

(C)   end with the closing of the sale and the delivery of the insurance policy

(D)   dictate that contact be maintained with the client until the policy matures or is terminated

READ THE FOLLOWING DIRECTIONS BEFORE CONTINUING

The questions below differ from the preceding questions in that they all contain the word EXCEPT. So you understand fully the basis used in selecting each answer, be sure to read each question carefully.

7.   The text states that marketing practices that financial services professionals (particularly those engaged in selling life insurance) should avoid include all of the following EXCEPT

(A)   false advertising

(B)   lack of full disclosure

(C)   the use of illustrations

(D)   unnecessary replacement

8.   Financial services professionals should document each of the following elements of every sale EXCEPT

(A)   the reason for the product recommendation

(B)   the illustration used as the basis of the sale

(C)   the discovery agreement

(D)   a disclosure statement

9.   Each of the following statements are among the keys to full disclosure EXCEPT

(A)   Provide your client with information about the product.

(B)   Provide your client with information about the company that is offering the product.

(C)   Provide your client with information about the illustration used in your sales presentation.

(D)   Provide your client with information regarding your role in the sales process.

10.   The text states that all of the following are steps in the sales presentation process EXCEPT

(A)   The agent selects one or two recommendations that best serve the client's needs.

(B)   The agent meets with his or her client and provides the recommendation(s).

(C)   The agent explains to the client the reasons behind the recommendation(s).

(D)   The agent allows the client time to think over the recommendation(s).

1. Identify the necessary steps for the proper use of computer-generated illustrations within the sales process.

2. Describe what circumstances constitute a replacement.

3. Explain when replacement is and is not an acceptable practice.

4. Describe what constitutes rebating.

5. List the key arguments for and against the legal use of rebating.

6. Describe the pros and cons of different forms of compensation.

MARKETPLACE PRACTICE ISSUES IN TODAY'S SELLING ENVIRONMENT

Challenges arise in any discussion of the ethics of the financial services profession, where the term "financial services professional" or "financial services industry" includes any of the group, such as insurance agents, broker-dealers and registered investment advisers. In many cases, each group is governed by a specific set of regulations and each practice raises its own specific ethical concerns and issues. In addition to the multiple roles played within the financial services industry, the industry is also distinguished from other professions for two reasons:

1. Financial services practitioners may provide good advice and suitable recommendations and assist their clients to implement their suggestions through facilitating the purchase of financial products. It is their role in the implementation phase which distinguishes them from other professionals, such as physicians and attorneys, who are typically only in the business of selling advice.

2. Financial service firms may act as an intermediary between financial services professionals and their clients, or at least as a third party,

which is involved in the transaction between the practitioner and the client. The firm has an ethical obligation to the well-being of the client, as well as obligations to the professionals they employ. The financial services professionals have an obligation of loyalty to their firm, as well as an obligation to look after the interests of their clients. As we have seen in previous chapters, at times, these obligations generate conflicting and incompatible duties.

Due to these factors, financial services professionals are likely to face ethical challenges, which other professionals will not confront. These challenges are particularly acute, since they are embedded within the structure of the industry itself. In this final chapter, we will consider some of the areas where ethical issues emerge from practices due to the unique structure of the financial services industry. They are:

- illustration issues
- rebating issues
- replacement issue
- compensation issues

ILLUSTRATIONS

In the life insurance industry, one of the prominent examples of misrepresentation and lack of disclosure is found in the misuse of illustrations. In selling insurance products, as well as some other financial products, the professional must provide illustrations of possible future gains or losses. Illustrations are a focal point in the ethics of financial services. Most financial advisors provide their clients with product illustrations prior to the close of a sale. Sales illustrations can be useful tools to demonstrate how a product works and they can help a client make an informed decision. However, they can be a source of ethical conflict. Rather than serving as a disclosure vehicle, illustrations can be improperly used as a vehicle that entices a client to buy, by distorting and misrepresenting the future operation of the financial product. Remind your clients that illustrations are not exact predictions of how a particular product's values will look in the future. Only guaranteed values are guaranteed.

ILLUSTRATION HISTORY AND EVOLUTION

In the life insurance industry, policy illustrations were fairly bland and standardized for many years. Illustrations were prepared by home office units and they showed estimated cash values and dividends on traditional whole life policies. The illustrations were fairly straightforward and represented a close approximation of what actually developed in future years.

Illustrations began to change in the 1980s. Technology became more sophisticated and facilitated the illustration of a greater range of variables. At the same time, the product portfolio began to change dramatically with the introduction of universal life insurance. At that time, life insurance began to be viewed as more than just insurance; it was now beginning to be viewed as an investment vehicle.

At that time, illustrations used historically high double-digit interest rates as the basis for projected values. These values were far in excess of policy guarantees. As long as interest rates remained high, no one seemed to notice the difference between what was projected and what was guaranteed. However, when interest rates began to fall, projected values did not hold up. Policy owners began receiving notices telling them of the need for increased or continued premiums. Consumers have used illustrations produced in the early 1980s, for example, as the basis of complaints that policies did not perform as expected. Agents began receiving angry letters from clients and their attorneys. There were charges of unethical behavior. Both individual agents and the insurers suffered tarnished reputations. Insurers spent billions of dollars to satisfy the claims of disgruntled policy owners.

Review Item: Time Crunch
Agent Myra Jones: "Joe, may I ask you a question?"
Client Joe Dunkirk: "I have no time. Just get me some coverage."
How would you respond?

ILLUSTRATIONS — THEIR COMPONENTS

Having a clear understanding of what an illustration is and what it is meant to accomplish is one way of avoiding future consumer dissatisfaction. This is why it is so important for financial advisors to explain the role and limitation of the insurance illustration to a client both before and after a sale is made.

Any illustration starts as a sheet of numbers indicating what is guaranteed and what is projected or what was achieved in the past. Some of the figures on the sheet are guaranteed by the issuing company, while other figures are not guaranteed.

We need to explain the variables behind illustrations to our clients. Dividend scales, credited interest rates and mortality charges are among the variables that should be discussed.

For example, a client must understand whether or not a company reserves the right to change mortality charges. The client must further understand the possible implications of such a change. If a world wide flu epidemic, such as the one of 1918, should occur with numerous ensuing deaths, policy mortality charges would likely rise. On the other hand, if the population continues to enjoy increased longevity, policy mortality charges are likely to remain stable or fall.

Clients who understand that an illustration is just that, an illustration, are less likely to file complaints or feel that they have made a wrong purchase decision. These clients also spread the word that insurance is a wise purchase. Such talk is good for the industry and good for our careers. In other words, by explaining the role of the illustration to a client, we are practicing good ethics that translates into good business.

ILLUSTRATION USE

Historically, it is the case that agents who sell insurance on the basis of illustrations alone are engaged in an unwise practice. Some financial services professionals have simply decided not to use illustrations as part of the sales process. However, based on the principle of honest forecasting, the NAIC Model Illustration Act, spells out in detail what can and cannot be done with illustrations, and requires that an insured receive an illustration at some point in the life insurance purchasing process.

Properly presented, illustrations are legitimate tools that help agents provide clients with full disclosure about the products being considered. Illustrations also provide agents with a documentation mechanism. Agents who choose not to use illustrations as part of the sales process close off two avenues that facilitate good marketplace practices. Consider the following points:

- Without an illustration, an agent runs the risk of forgetting to disclose important information. For example, a client may not realize that there are guaranteed and nonguaranteed elements involved in policy performance. Several years after the sale, the client may discover this on his or her own and become dissatisfied.
- An agent who sells without an illustration loses an opportunity to obtain important documentation of good marketplace practices

for his or her files. If there was no illustration used during the presentation, there is no illustration for the client to sign and no file indicating exactly what was shown or discussed.

Although the use of illustrations in the sales process can be very helpful, it is important to emphasize that a decision to purchase a financial product cannot be made by simply reviewing the numbers on a ledger. There must be a need for the product. Before a final purchase decision is made, today's client will seek information regarding the company that sells the product. In other words, you should be prepared to provide your clients with information regarding the history of your company and its financial strength from two or three independent rating services. You should also be prepared to explain why this particular policy or product is suitable for them and will help the client meet his or her financial goals.

MODEL REGULATIONS ON ILLUSTRATIONS

As noted, The National Association of Insurance Commissioners (NAIC) has recently promulgated model regulations on this subject. These regulations basically call for clients to be supplied with illustrations showing current assumptions, together with more conservative assumptions developed under the technical aspects of the Model's guidelines and the Actuarial Standards Board.

Until your state adopts these new NAIC regulations, it is probably prudent to provide your client with illustrations showing the following:

- guaranteed values
- current return values
- current return values minus one percent—or, to be even more conservative, 2 percent (this guideline applies to newer-type interest or investment-sensitive policies)

The NAIC Life Insurance Illustrations Model Regulation provides that the insurer's illustrated scale be used with the nonguaranteed element, reduced as follows:

- dividends at 50 percent of the current dividends contained in the illustrated scale used
- nonguaranteed credited interest at rates that are the average of the guaranteed rates and the current rates contained in the illustrated scale used

- all nonguaranteed charges, including but not limited to, term insurance charges and mortality and expense charges, at rates that are the average of the guaranteed rates and the current rates contained in the illustrated scale used

This takes time to explain. However, this type of client education pays off. Clients begin to anticipate how changes in interest rates can affect their cash values and premiums. If an unscrupulous agent follows you illustrating exaggerated returns, your clients will be able to spot the difference and your business is far more likely to remain on the books.

ILLUSTRATIONS AND POLICY COMPARISONS

Some agents try to compare policies based on illustrations. Are such comparisons valid? Probably not—it's like comparing apples and oranges. Such illustrations are designed to show how a particular product of a particular company works. These illustrations are not suitable for comparing the product of one company with the product of another. There are too many variables, and the variables are inconsistent from company to company. Policy selection starts with knowledge of the insurance product and analysis of the assumptions underlying each policy. Policies should be selected on criteria that include each company's financial circumstances and the quality of service. Other factors involved in policy selection include the quality and availability of service offered by the individual financial advisor representing the company.

Documentation of Illustration Use

You need to document your illustration work. We recommend that you use the company's illustration formats. In addition, we recommend that you take (to the policy delivery) three copies of the illustration used to close the sale. At that point, you and the client should sign all three illustration copies. Give one signed copy to the client. Retain one signed copy for your records. Finally, use one signed copy as a disclosure statement to be turned into the insurance carrier. The policy owner would acknowledge having read the policy illustration and noting the nonguaranteed elements. Agents verify that they have explained both the guaranteed and nonguaranteed elements of the policy. As more and more states adopt the NAIC Life Insurance Illustrations Model Regulation, this final step will become a mandatory element of the selling process.

These steps provide evidence of the illustration specifically used for the insurance policy, should any questions arise in the future. Further, these steps stress to the client the importance of understanding just what an illustration is and what it is not.

Regulation of Illustrations for Specialized Policies

Many insurance professionals meet client needs with a variety of specialized products. These include blended policies, second-to-die policies, and senior citizen policies. The illustrations prepared for these policies require particular attention to client education and ethical concerns. What follows are some suggestions about the obligations we have in presenting and selling these types of products.

Blended Policies

Blended policies are combinations of permanent insurance and term riders. These policies serve the needs of many individuals who require high amounts of coverage, but cannot currently afford to pay permanent insurance rates. The blended policy solves this problem by locking in insurability at an affordable cost. Clients who purchase these policies must be educated as to their components and the implications of those components.

Second-to-Die Policies

These policies are designed to pay a death benefit at the death of the second insured. Clients must be educated to the fact that, although both parties may be insured, there is no payment at the first insured's death. Changes that occur in the policies at the first death should also be clarified.

Another sensitive issue involves what happens to the policy in the case of a divorce of insured parties. Clearly explain your company's policies. As we have suggested before, documentation is frequently important to demonstrate the thoroughness of your business practices. Follow up your discussions of these policy provisions with a letter enclosing explanatory materials provided by your company.

Senior Citizen Policies

Some insurance professionals sell policies aimed at the over-age-60 seniors market. These policies frequently limit the level of death benefits during a period following the inception date of the policy. Sometimes, these policies are designed so that accumulated premiums exceed policy death benefits during the first 10 years when the policy is in force. If you sell such a policy, be aware that the NAIC model disclosure law specifies that the policy owner must be given a free look of 30 days. This is longer than the ordinary 10-day free-look period. In addition, you are required to provide the senior policy owner with a special insurance guide. NAIC Model Regulations also specify that a policy financial review form be provided to a client.

Universal Life Policies

The NAIC has drafted model legislation that applies to universal life products. The NAIC specifies that purchasers of universal life be supplied with a special statement of policy information. The aim here is to alert the policy owner to the fact that he or she has bought a universal life product and not a traditional whole life product. Whether or not your state has currently adopted the NAIC model legislation, follow its overall dictates and educate your client about the differences between universal life insurance and traditional life insurance.

Annuity Products

The NAIC has endorsed a new Annuity Disclosure Model Regulation. The purpose of this regulation is to provide standards for the disclosure of a certain minimal amount of information about annuity contracts to protect consumers and foster consumer education. The regulation specifies the minimum information that must be disclosed and the method for disclosing it in connection with the sale of annuity contracts. The goal of the regulation is to ensure that purchasers of annuity contracts understand certain basic features of annuity contracts.

You may find compliance with these guidelines cumbersome. Keep in mind, however, that the guidelines protect not only policy owners but also financial services professionals. Financial advisors who follow these guidelines demonstrate and provide proof of ethical behavior.

REPLACEMENT AND REBATING

In addition to misrepresentation, lack of disclosure, and misuse of illustrations, there are two other significant practices that are subject to ethical abuse and need to be examined: replacement and rebating.

Replacement

Replacement is a very broad term. It means more than just substituting one life insurance policy or annuity contract for another that was issued earlier. It includes situations where existing life insurance policy or annuity benefits are terminated or modified in conjunction with the purchase of a new life insurance policy or annuity, or where existing life policy or annuity values are used to fund a new life policy or annuity. Replacement is usually not in the best interest of a client.

Review Item: Application Information

Client Molly Fenwick: "Why do you need to know all this information? I like my privacy."

How would you respond?

The chief ethical rule is this: Policy replacement should always be focused on the best interest of the client. Careful compliance with state regulations is one way of ensuring that both you and the client have the information necessary to decide whether the replacement is in his or her best interest. The new policy should be based on the client's needs, and it is prudent to document the specific needs satisfied by the new insurance. If replacement is appropriate, the transaction should be done as a tax-free exchange under Section 1035 of the Internal Revenue Code so it remains tax favored.

Replacement versus Twisting

Many financial services professionals are familiar with the term twisting, but twisting and replacement are often confused. Replacement is legal and in many cases, ethical; twisting is not.

Twisting is an unnecessary replacement of a product to benefit the financial advisor or the broker. It occurs when a financial advisor induces a client to drop existing coverage, without clearly explaining the benefits that will be lost under the old policy. In addition, there is often a failure to reveal the new costs involved with taking out a new policy or the effect of new policy coverage on access to cash values. In other words, twisting can be considered a form of misrepresentation. In most cases, it is motivated by financial advisors seeking commission dollars.

Twisting can be external or internal. Agents may unethically replace policies sold by other companies or replace old policies issued by their own carrier in prior years.

Piggybacking is another type of replacement activity. It is the practice of using existing policy values, whether through a loan, dividend withdrawal, or partial or full cash surrender, to fund a new policy. Like twisting, piggybacking can be illegal and unethical.

NAIC REPLACEMENT GUIDELINES

In recognition of the potential abuses that surround replacements, the NAIC drafted a Life Insurance and Annuities Replacement Model Regulation that most states have adopted. The model requires a financial advisor who is replacing a product to comply with detailed disclosure rules in order to protect policy owner interests.

The disclosure rules require that the policy owner be provided with enough information to make a comparison between current and proposed coverage. The rules first require the insurance professional to make a determination about whether or not replacement is involved in a particular sales situation. That may sound simple, but replacement is a complex concept.

The NAIC defines replacement as follows:

> Replacement means a transaction in which a new policy or contract is to be purchased, and it is known or should be known to the proposing producer, or to the proposing insurer if there is no producer, that by reason of the transaction, an existing policy or contract has been or is to be:
>
> - lapsed, forfeited, surrendered or partially surrendered, assigned to the replacing insurer or otherwise terminated;
> - converted to reduced paid-up insurance, continued as extended term insurance, or otherwise reduced in value by the use of nonforfeiture benefits or other policy values;
> - amended so as to effect either reduction in benefits or in the term for which coverage would otherwise remain in force or which benefits would be paid;
> - reissued with any reduction in cash value; or
> - loans used to finance the purchase of a new policy.

If, in fact, replacement is involved, the financial advisor must provide the policy owner with a special form. This form is called *Notice Regarding Replacement*.

The Notice Regarding Replacement form enables policy owners to obtain up-to-date information on their existing coverage in order to compare it with newly proposed coverage. In addition, the NAIC model regulation provides for notification of the proposed replacement to the existing carrier. Where external replacement is involved, this encourages policy owners to confer with representatives of their current carrier. Where internal replacement is involved, this helps to assure compliance with internal company rules.

The replacement compliance rules protect both the consumer and the financial services professional. If a replacement does, in fact, occur, its reasons and justification will be clearly documented.

Producers should remember that they are vulnerable to legal action for damages should they fail to disclose to the client any material consequences of a replacement transaction, such as a decrease in coverage, loss of cash value or an increase in premium. Producers should also keep in mind that failure to comply with state insurance laws and regulations can result in fines, license suspension or termination. Additionally, material misrepresentation or nondisclosure in the context of a replacement transaction involving an equity product, such as a variable life policy, can constitute violation of the securities laws.

EXAMPLES OF INAPPROPRIATE REPLACEMENT

No two life insurance clients have the exact same goals or financial needs. Therefore, applying one set of rules to fit all situations is virtually impossible when deciding whether or not to make a replacement. Here, however, are some examples of when replacement may be inappropriate.

1. *First-Year Commission.* Your client obtained coverage several years ago from a highly rated company. The policy cash values are building. The client has just broken even between premium dollars and cash values. You can offer a slightly different policy, and full commissions will be payable. Cash value that the client has built up will be consumed in meeting initial costs of the new policy. The numbers show the new policy is simply not cost effective in comparison with the established coverage.

2. *Suicide and Incontestable Provisions.* Your client has a policy that has been in force for 5 years. Contestability provisions have already been met. Your client's father had a history of severe depression requiring, at one point, institutionalization. This concerns your client. Replacement means starting suicide and contestable periods anew.

3. *Declining Health.* Your client took out a policy several years ago, at standard rates. Since that time, he has had heart surgery. New coverage would come with a high rating.

4. *Increasing Age.* Your client took out a policy when she was 30 years old. It is 10 years later, and the premium for the same coverage has increased over time.

5. *Attractive Loan Rates.* Your client's current coverage provides her with the ability to borrow against cash values at a 5 percent guaranteed loan rate. She has borrowed and repaid loans several times. The face value of the policy, however, is inadequate to meet her needs. Your initial suggestion was to replace this coverage, but a better solution would be to write new, additional coverage.

6. *Adverse Tax Consequences.* Many times, a client considers replacing a policy that has large, outstanding loans. The law does permit the income-tax-free exchange of one life insurance policy for another.

   However, if a policy loan is not carried over from the old policy to the new one, the loan is not part of the income-tax-free exchange. This can lead to adverse tax consequences. Your client has a large loan outstanding on her policy, which she does not wish to currently repay. Your company will not roll over the loan. Your best course of action is to tell your client to get specific advice on the tax consequences.

To sum up: If you are going to replace a client's policy, make sure it is in the client's best interest. That means you have to evaluate all of the pros and cons of the replacement activity. To replace a life insurance policy, simply to generate commissions for yourself is the height of unethical behavior for the financial services professional.

REBATING

Another practice that comes under fire in the insurance industry is the practice of rebating. Rebating is an effective sales tool in many areas, such as an automobile dealer offering a rebate when selling a car. But the situation is different in selling life insurance. While rebating was common practice during the 20th century, it was largely banned in most states as a result of the Armstrong Commission findings, which stated that rebating was "considered to be contrary to the maintenance of fair competition and equity among policy owners."[27] The prohibition against rebating raises interesting is an example of the attempt of regulation to strike a balance between promoting market efficiency through expanding the freedom to contract and establishing a fair and level playing field for both agents and consumers.

In selling life insurance, rebating involves reducing the premium or giving some other valuable consideration not specified in the policy to the buyer as an inducement to purchase the insurance. The classic rebate situation involves a financial advisor giving back a portion of his or her commission that reduces the first premium in order to induce the prospect to insure.

PROS AND CONS OF LAWS PROHIBITING REBATING

Why would there be opposition to rebating? Financial advisors generally tend to view rebates as unwarranted pressure on their compensation. They also believe that widespread rebating would adversely affect both the insurance-consuming public and insurers in several ways, including the following.

Why Rebating Should Not Be Allowed

1. *Rebating Would Be Unfair.* Rebating would result in varying first-year charges to similarly situated policy owners, thereby fostering unfair discrimination against those consumers not possessing either economic leverage to demand rebates (that is, purchasers of small amounts of coverage) or the knowledge to do so. If forced to make rebates in selected situations to meet the competition, financial advisors would be forced to demand higher commissions from their insurers in order to make a living. Eventually, such increased commissions would work their way back into the cost of the product, which would result in higher premiums

---

27. Burke A. Christensen, "An Analysis of Life Insurance Rebating Process: Is it Helpful or Harmful?" *Trusts and Estates.* September 1991: 56.

across the board for policy owners, many of whom would be unable to demand and obtain rebates.

2. *Rebating Has an Adverse Impact on Companies' Financial Condition*. Further, permitting rebates could lead to the ruinous competition that initiated the ban in the first place, nearly 100 years ago. Intense competition through rebates may adversely impact the financial condition of insurers (perhaps to the point of insolvency). This could be rooted in increased early year lapse rates resulting from replacements, thereby preventing insurers from recovering issue expenses normally amortized over several years. Weakened financial conditions also could emerge from the pressure on the insurer to raise commission rates to enable financial advisors to compete, even though the insurer might be unable to raise premiums to recover the increased expenses because of competition in the marketplace.

3. *It Leads to Unnecessary Replacements*. Rebates afford a powerful tool for those financial advisors inclined to replace policies. Utilizing the lure of rebates, an agent can more easily encourage a policy owner to replace his or her existing policy, thereby incurring the expensive burden of another set of acquisition costs. In situations where replacement is not warranted in terms of policy owner interest, the availability of rebating exacerbates the replacement problem.

4. *Causes Shortage of Financial Advisors and Creates Adverse Public Effects*. Larger agencies and more established financial advisors tend to be better positioned to offer significant rebates. Consequently, the removal of the ban on rebating would encourage the concentration of agency forces, would favor the more established financial advisors, and would result in increased turnover of financial advisors, especially new ones who already have a difficult time surviving long enough to develop a viable career. In turn, these impacts could aggravate the shortage of financial advisors in life insurance agencies, thereby reducing the number of financial advisors available to service the public and limiting competition in the marketplace. Furthermore, in view of the generally held axiom that life insurance is sold rather than bought, the fewer the number of financial advisors, the smaller the amount of life insurance sales and, in turn, the greater number of under insured in this nation's population.

5. *Weakens Quality of Policy Owner Decision Making*. The availability of rebates detracts from the likelihood of prospective policy owners making the best decisions for themselves in purchasing long-term

contracts of life insurance. Encouraging prospective buyers to focus on the size of the rebates in the first year (a very small portion of the total cost of insurance over the life of the policy) will tend to reduce the quality of buyer discernment in comparing prices. Perhaps the gravest danger posed by rebating is the all-too-real possibility that the buyers will be more influenced by the size of the rebate, that is, by the "deal" they can make, than by the merits of the insurance contract, the total long-range costs, the nature and suitability of the products and the quality of the financial advisor's counseling and service.

6. *Customer Initiated Churning.* Depending on what form the rebate takes, consumers may be attracted to "new and better deals" and allow a policy to lapse or exchange it for a new policy in order to enjoy additional benefits. This would increase the cost of insurance as the cost to write the policy may exceed the first year premium undermining the financial stability. This short term strategy may backfire with an unanticipated change in their health or lifestyle, which may make it harder for the consumer to get the same coverage and the same price the next time around.

Why Rebating Should Be Allowed

Despite these public policy arguments, the 1980s witnessed increasing agitation for the elimination of the ban against rebating. The critics of anti-rebate laws maintain the following.

1. *Laws Against Rebating Are Anti-competitive.* The rebate laws are anti-competitive by needlessly sheltering financial advisors from competition, thereby contributing to excessive insurance costs. Consumer opportunity to negotiate between financial advisors for a better price is barred. In contrast, the removal of the ban on rebates will focus on competition for the consumers' business, rather than insurers simply competing for financial advisors to market their products. Permitting rebates would contribute to lower costs, for at least some consumers.

2. *Rebating Permits Less Competent Financial Advisors to Compete While Consumers Pay More.* In stifling competition between financial advisors, the ban on rebates permits the less competent or inefficient ones to be compensated on a basis equivalent to that of those who are the most knowledgeable and efficient. The absence of competition reduces incentives for providing superior service. The essence of negotiated commissions is the ability of the consumer to purchase the amount and quality of services desired

and needed. In contrast, under the fixed-commission system, the consumer may obtain a particular service only by paying for the full range of services the financial advisor offers. Whether the consumer wants, needs, or actually utilizes the financial advisor's services does not affect the price paid.

3. *Rebate-Caused Discrimination is Not Unfair.* Rebating does not give rise to unfair discrimination. The life insurance business is replete with examples of discrimination. (Remember, it is only unfair discrimination that is prohibited.) Economies of size garner better rates. Insurers discriminate in underwriting by allocating policy owners to different rate classifications. Group insurance policy owners enjoy the lower costs associated with the absence of the high first-year commissions paid on individual policy sales. Financial advisors discriminate in selecting their prospects.

4. *The Amount and Quality of Service.* Similarly, buyers should be able to select from among several financial advisors and vary their costs based on the amount and quality of work performed by them. A knowledgeable buyer who needs little prospecting, analysis, or research should not be compelled to pay the same commission as a difficult customer who utilizes far more of the financial advisor's time.

The question as to whether the anti-rebating regulations should be repealed is closely tied to questions of compensation disclosure discussed later in this chapter. Some commentators argue that if agents are required by a new state or federal regulation to disclose the amount they receive in commission for a particular product, the pressure to offer some form of rebate to consumers will increase. There is a concern that if more specific compensation disclosure was mandated without permitting the agent to negotiate this amount with his or her client, the agent would be placed in an untenable position. If agents are pressured to make some sort of accommodation to their clients, illegal rebating may increase and unscrupulous agents who are willing to violate the law would benefit at the expense of other more ethical agents. Even if agents are not required to make a more specific disclosure, given the increasing awareness of consumers of agent compensation (particularly through discount, online insurance brokers) it is quite likely that consumer pressure on traditional, full-service agents and issuing companies will compel agents and issuing companies to deal with this question at some time in the future.

In conclusion, like many of the ethical issues we have seen so far, the question of rebating poses two values in stark contrast— the value of the freedom to contract and the value of an expansion of the free market versus establishing a "level playing field" in which like consumers are treated in like ways and disadvantaged or vulnerable consumers are afforded protections against discrimination and unfair treatment. The importance of the values at stake mean that this debate is not likely to resolved soon.

Pros & Cons of Laws Against Rebating
Pros
• unfair discrimination
• adverse impact on insurer financial condition
• unnecessary replacements
• agent manpower shortage
• quality of policyholder decision making
Cons
• anticompetition
• absence of significant impact on insurer financial condition
• lack of inappropriate discrimination
• the amount and quality of service

CURRENT STATUS OF THE REGULATION OF REBATES

Florida and California are commonly know as "rebating" states, which means that a qualified insurance agency can rebate a portion of the purchase price back to the consumer. However, several life insurers in California have taken the position that it is within their right to refuse to deal with agents who do rebate. The California insurance department moved against insurers who fired an agent who offered his customers commission rebates. An administrative law judge concluded that it is not an unfair business practice for life insurers to do so. Although initially indicating that he would not accept the judge's ruling, the insurance commissioner ultimately concluded that insurers may fire agents who rebate. As a result, Proposition 103 repealed the prohibition against rebates. Insurers may fire those financial advisors who engage in such practices, if doing so constitutes a violation of their agency contracts with the insurer.

Elsewhere, to date, the arguments and influence of the proponents of the ban against rebating have prevailed in both public policy forums and judicial challenges. The other 48 states have roughly the same statues that bar agents from offering any benefit or discount (rebate) that induces the purchase of insurance. Unless change should be compelled at the federal level, it appears that the anti-rebate provision will remain the law in the vast majority of states at least for the immediate future. While rebating in Florida and California is legal, the legal climate remains hostile.

COMPENSATION ISSUES

The multitude of compensation models within the financial services industry is unique and distinguishes this industry from other professions. According to one practitioner, "In fact, it's difficult to think of another profession in which the consumer pays in so many different ways for services."[28] The issue of how compensation systems ought to be designed to incentivize ethical behavior within the financial services industry is influenced by two distinguishing characteristics:

1. The duty of care financial services professionals owe to their clients. This issue refers to the three-part relationship within the financial services industry, and how a particular profession is able to balance these conflicting loyalties and obligations.
2. The fact that many financial services professionals both provide advice and sell products and services.

In the financial services industry, there is knowledge asymmetry. Financial services professionals are experts in financial instruments and, by and large, have an advisory role to play with their clients. This gives them informational power, which provides them with a distinct advantage in their interactions with clients and potential clients. Not only does the advisor possess more information than the client, but the advisor is also in a position to determine what information to share with his or her client. Since clients "do not know what they don't know," the advisor can use or misuse this power in influencing the decisions of their clients.

Clients value this expertise and seek out financial planning professionals in order to have access to information they do not currently possess. Clients rely on this information and expertise to make decisions that are in their best interest and are willing to compensate their financial services professional well in return for his or her advice and recommendations. The advice provided includes items such as what is a suitable transaction (such as a

---

28. Nancy Opiela, "The Future of Fees," *Journal of Financial Planning* (2006): 24.

suitable life insurance policy) or on a broader scale (such as the development of a comprehensive financial plan). In either case, given the informational power possessed by the financial services professional, it is necessary that this advice represents the best interests of the client.

But how should financial professionals be compensated for this advice? It is possible to develop a scale in which the we can show the different kinds of compensation and discuss what role those different forms should play in compensating for different types of financial services.

Different Types of Compensation Systems

At one end of the compensation progression are financial services professionals, who are compensated on the basis of a fee-only model. Fee-only providers do not receive commissions on the products they sell and are compensated solely on the basis of the advice they provide. Fee-only providers can be compensated in three different ways:

1. assets under management (AUM)
2. flat fee/retainer
3. hourly rates

Some practitioners operate under a model which is a combination of these forms. An example is charging an hourly rate or a flat fee/retainer to develop a comprehensive financial plan for a client, and then charging a percentage of the assets under management for investment management services. In the AUM model, compensation is tied directly to the value of the investments the professional oversees and manages on behalf of the client. A flat rate or retainer model is a flat fee which covers all of the services related to the client's planning needs and account. Unlike the AUM model, the fee does not fluctuate with asset performance. However, the retainer charged can vary, depending on the size of the account or other factors. In other words, a flat fee or retainer approach does not signify a "one-price" for all clients approach. In many cases, the retainer fee is fixed for a set time period and then renegotiated, dependent on the needs of the client and the professional. Under the hourly rate model, the financial services professional charges clients on the basis of time spent working for the client.

At the other end of the spectrum are providers, who are only paid a commission on the products they sell by the issuers of those products. Commission-only providers are paid a commission by the issuer of the company which is built in to the price of the financial product purchased by the consumer. Providers are compensated directly by the issuing company and only indirectly by their clients.

There are three options which fall between fee-only and commission-only providers on the progression above.

1. Combination fee/commission providers charge their clients a fee for the consultation and the preparation of a financial plan, and may also receive a commission from the sale of recommended products purchased during the implementation phase.

2. Fee-offset providers charge a fee for developing a financial plan for potential clients, but this fee can be offset or discounted if the client purchases financial products for which the professional receives commission paid by the issuer of the products.

3. Salaried providers are compensated by means of a salary which is paid by the financial services firm by which they are employed. The salary model can also include a bonus component, if the professional reaches certain sales goals and targets.

Relative Advantages and Disadvantages of Different Compensation Models

Each of the compensation models represented has advantages and disadvantages, and there is no compensation model which is suitable for every client. While the commission based model is often singled out for criticism, it is important to note that each of the compensation models on the scale has its own particular conflicts of interest. The assets under management model is frequently touted as a "conflict-free" compensation model because it aligns the interests of the professional with the interests of the client. Quite simply, the financial services professional's compensation increases (or decreases) in proportion to the growth (or losses) in the client's account. Since the professional is compensated solely on the basis of account performance, clients can be more confident that their advisor is only recommending financial products or strategies which are in their the best interest. As we have mentioned throughout this book, *trust and confidence in the professional* is the foundation for a profitable and productive relationship between a client and his or her financial advisor. AUM may work to bolster this confidence by not only aligning the interests of the client and his or her advisor, but also by removing the perception of a conflict of interest. There are many commission-based financial services professionals who would never recommend an unsuitable product, regardless of the material benefit to themselves. However, the mere *possibility of the temptation* may make it more difficult for some clients to trust a commission-based professional.

To the extent that the AUM model mitigates this apparent temptation and, perhaps more importantly, the distrust that the existence of the temptation creates in the client, is an advantage. However, the AUM model also presents a unique set of ethical challenges. A potential conflict concerns situations in which the interests of the practitioner and the client are not aligned. Their interests may diverge in cases in which it is in the best interest of clients to move assets out of their account. For example, a client may be looking to diversify his or her portfolio through purchasing tangible assets (such as real estate or art), improve liquidity through increasing cash reserves or purchasing life or long-term care insurance.[29] Since fee-based advisors are compensated on the basis of the amount of assets they manage, fee-based advisors have an interest in maintaining (and increasing) the total amount of capital managed for the client.

A second concern arises from compensation being tied to the growth of the client's account. Compensation is then subject to fluctuations which are beyond the control of the professional. For example, if the stock market is performing extremely well and the value of the account increases by 26 percent, the client may wonder what exactly the professional did to warrant such a pay increase. On the other hand, if an advisor has little to do with the gains in bull market, he or she also is not responsible for the losses which accumulate in a bear market. The crux of the issue is that AUM model does not appear to compensate an adviser on the basis of his expertise and/or skill. The consequence is that professionals may be rewarded too much in times of economic prosperity and penalized harshly in times of downturn and recession. This may strike some people as unfair, since compensation is not explicitly tied to merit and skill, but can depend on the vagaries of the market.

Flat Fee Model and Hourly Models

Under the flat-fee model (also referred to as a retainer) an amount is agreed upon by the advisor and client. This amount usually based on the client's net worth, rather than the value of the portfolio, and is paid in quarterly

---

29. John Robinson, "Who's the Fairest of Them All? A Comparative Analysis of Financial Advisor Compensation Models." *Journal of Financial Planning* Vol. 20 No. 5 (May 2007): 58.

installments.[30] The hourly-rate model is usually applied by financial services professionals engaged by clients to work on one or two specific issues, rather than developing a comprehensive financial plan or strategy. An advantage of the flat fee model is that since the compensation is tied specifically to the perceived value of the advice provided (and not to the quantity or performance of products sold), it is possible for the advisor to be more objective in his or her recommendations. Specifically, the flat fee model does not suffer from the problems regarding allocations and diversification strategies which may occur under the AUM model. Since the flat fee advisor is not compensated on the basis of the portfolio, but on the net worth of the client, the interests of the advisor and the client remain more closely aligned in a variety of circumstances. As was the case in the AUM model, the alignment of interests may make clients more comfortable with the recommendations of their financial advisor, and encourage the trust and confidence which is essential to a profitable and productive relationship.

Like each of the models under consideration, the flat-fee model raises a unique set of potential difficulties. As with attorneys, who also use the flat-fee model (retainers), shirking may occur. Shirking basically means doing the minimum of work necessary to maintain the relationship. In the flat-fee model, the advisor's compensation is not tied explicitly to the products sold or portfolio growth. Therefore, the advisor is not incentivized to pursue opportunities which may be in the best interest of their clients. In an article published in the *Financial Planning Journal*, it was suggested that: "If a flat fee advisor recommends few investment changes from one year to the next, the question may arise whether this lack of change is due to a belief that the portfolio remains sound or due to shirking on the part of the advisor."[31] This concern is exacerbated by the *information asymmetry* between an advisor and his or her clients, which makes it difficult for the client to assess the value of the advisor's advice and recommendations.

Hourly-fee plans offer an important advantage, in that this model makes it possible for financial services providers to work with clients at all points on the income scale. It also allows clients to seek out financial advisors to resolve a particular problem, rather than paying for services they do not need or want. The hourly-fee model is perhaps the most transparent of each

---

30. John Robinson, "Who's the Fairest of Them All? A Comparative Analysis of Financial Advisor Compensation Models." *Journal of Financial Planning* Vol. 20 No. 5 (May 2007): 59.
31. John Robinson, "Who's the Fairest of Them All? A Comparative Analysis of Financial Advisor Compensation Models." *Journal of Financial Planning* Vol. 20 No. 5 (May 2007): 60.

of the models on the progression, which can be a tremendous advantage. Clients understand how much they are paying for services and can make decisions concerning what level and type of service they are willing to pay for or can afford. The difficulties with the hourly rate model are similar to those found within the flat-fee/retainer model of compensation; namely, shirking. However, these concerns may be mitigated by the fact that clients often engage an hourly-fee advisor to perform a clearly delineated objective or accomplish a specific task. Therefore, it is easier to determine a time line for completion and whether it was completed in a satisfactory manner. Given the information asymmetry between the client and professional, concerns may emerge regarding "over billing." Additionally, concerns may arise regarding what is referred to as "value billing," versus hourly billing. For example, Eliza, an hourly-fee financial advisor, was recently engaged by a client for a specific project. Eliza spends 40 hours developing a template which will allow her to complete the service promised to her client. She knows that she will be able to use this template repeatedly in the future. If another client engages Eliza for exactly the same service as the original client, it will only take Eliza 6 hours to complete the work. How much should Eliza bill the first client? How much should Eliza bill the second client? This is a thorny issue which involves important concerns over fairness.

Commission-based Model

The commission-based model is the original form of compensation for many financial services providers. The commission-based system emerged as a response to the three-part relationship between financial services institutions (intermediaries), professionals and clients. As we discussed in chapter 4, relationships within the financial services profession can be understood through the framework of agency-theory, in which the interests of a principal are represented by their agent. Concerns about the commission based model revolve around the idea that a commission-based system functions to align the interest of the professional with only one of their principals, namely, the firm by which they are employed or the issuing company of the product they are selling. "It (the commission-based model) effectively motivates firms and sales people alike because it aligns a firm's interest in increasing revenues with a salesperson's desire to maximize income."[32]

---

32. Jim Settel and Nancy B. Kurland, "Can We Create a Conflict-Free Commission Payment System" *Business and Society Review* 100/101 (1998): 35.

This misalignment of interests is exacerbated by the fact that the client may not be aware of their advisor's other obligations. Under the commission-based model, practitioners are compensated on the quantity of products they sell, and not on the quality of these products or suitability of these products to meet the needs of their clients. Within this model, practitioners materially benefit from selling products with a higher commission and there can be little material incentive for practitioners to recommend products that are the most suitable for their clients. The focus on quantity of products sold can tempt practitioners with an incentive to engage in churning, which involves instigating empty transactions in order to generate commissions, for the practitioner, without benefiting the client at all.

The time delay between when the practitioner is compensated for the sale and when the client realizes the value of the product also creates a conflict of interests. Under most commission based models, practitioners receive their commission shortly after they complete the transaction with the client. On the other hand, it can be months, or even years, before clients see the value (or the harm) of the financial product they purchased.

While the commission-based model has received some negative press in recent decades, many defend this model for several reasons. The first is that it creates a system of motivated practitioners incentivized to sell "hard-to-sell" products. And secondly, the commission-based model creates options for these consumers to act in their own interest. The mere existence of a conflict of interest, such as varying commissions, does not mean that practitioner will exploit these conflicts in order to materially benefit themselves at the expense of their clients. Further, it is certainly possible to develop compensation systems which better align the interests of the practitioner and the interests of the client.

The Importance of Compensation Disclosure

To sum up compensation, start with the knowledge that there are several different compensation models available to financial services practitioners and consumers. The variety of options is an advantage because it enables consumers to select which model best meets their needs, and enables them to pay for the amount of advice they believe is appropriate. In order for consumers to realize the benefits of being able to select from a multitude of compensation models, financial services practitioners should be forthright about how they are paid.

Ethical Issues in Compensation—How Much Disclosure Is Enough?

How much detail is necessary for professionals to provide to clients regarding their compensation? After the practitioner discloses the compensation model to the client, is the practitioner required to discuss the exact amount of their compensation, and in what manner the compensation payments are disbursed? Do consumers have a right to know exactly how much commission a practitioner will make from the sale of a particular product? Some argue that full disclosure is not ethically required and, in fact, mandated full and complete disclosure could undermine the relationship between a professional and his or her clients. They argue that the commission-based compensation model developed as a response to the unique pressures of the life insurance industry, namely, the agency model which makes it unprofitable to offer full-time, salaried employment to all of their new agents. Opponents of detailed disclosure argue that, since the model has been institutionalized within the life insurance industry, many life insurance professionals have chosen a career which affords them relatively more control over the income than is possible in other professions and would therefore resist changing to a different compensation model. Finally, while professionals may receive a generous commission on the sale of a product, it is difficult to explain to the average consumer that this commission payment may be the only significant form of compensation he or she receives for that sale, which may have taken a great deal of time to complete. All of these factors make it difficult for the average consumer to understand the compensation model.

The guiding ethical principle should be to give the client enough information to make an informed decision on their own. That builds trust and helps build a profitable long term relationship. After all, as we have said throughout this book, good ethics is good business.

MUTUAL FUND FEES

Consumers and regulators have shown increasing concern regarding perceived conflicts of interest between fund investors and the companies and the companies, and individuals that market and distribute mutual fund shares. Most mutual funds are created and managed by a mutual fund management company, which is registered as an investment adviser with the SEC. Management companies often offer a complex of funds with various investment objectives. Regulations mandate that the assets in any particular mutual fund must be insulated from those of other mutual funds in the same complex and from the operations and associated risks of the management company and other firms that provide services to the fund. Since the 1940 Investment Companies Act prohibits a mutual fund from acting as a distributor of its own assets, except under certain circumstances, mutual funds are required to look elsewhere to find distributors for their products.

Mutual funds sell shares in two ways: the first is exclusively through broker-dealers and the second is through unaffiliated brokers. Funds sold through brokers assess a sales load. A front-end load is a commission paid to the broker at the time the investor purchases the share. A back-end load is a commission paid to the broker when the investor sells the shares. The fund determines the load and the broker cannot negotiate a change the load with the customer. There are a myriad of other fees which attach to the purchase, holding and divesting of mutual fund shares. The popularity of mutual funds and the increasing dependence of many Americans on these investments, in order to ensure their retirement income, makes ethical practice in selling them crucially important. Reports on unethical behavior on the part of the management companies and brokers are troubling. While some actions are clearly illegal, such as the allowing of late-market trading when this is expressly prohibited by the prospectus, there are other policies in which the moral status is not so clear. One of these issues concerns the moral appropriateness of 12b-1 fees.

12b-1 Fees

12b-1 fees are named after an SEC rule that allows funds to pass along costs associated with marketing and distribution to the shareholders. The original justification for the introduction of 12b-1 fees was to attract new shareholders into the fund through advertising, and providing incentives to brokers to sell the fund shares.[33] Shareholders would benefit since the expansion of the fund creates an economy of scale which would reduce the expense burden of the shareholders. In other words, a greater number of fund investors would proportionately diminish the amount of expenses required of each fund investor. Therefore, 12b-1 fees were originally considered "cost-neutral." When rule 12b-1 was adopted in 1980, it was generally assumed that the primary users of 12b-1 fees would be newer funds which needed to incentivize brokers to sell their shares, and smaller funds which needed to

---

33. Walsh, 2005 cited in Todd Houge and Jay Wellman, "The Use and Abuse of Mutual Fund Expenses" *Journal of Business Ethics* (2007) Vol. 70: 25.

increase in size in order to decrease the expense burden borne by their fund holders. In both cases, fund expansion would render the funds more competitive.[34]

However, the 12b-1 fees have been applied to achieve different objectives since their institution in 1980 and are now used less frequently to pay for advertising and marketing of the fund. More often, 12b-1 fees are now used as an alternative or in combination with sales loads as a means of compensating brokers for selling fund shares and as a way to compensate brokers for servicing accounts.[35]

When approving Rule 12b-1, the SEC acknowledged the fee, which allowed management companies to shift the expense of the marketing and distribution to the fund investors, may create a conflict of interest. The conflict emerges since *managers and investors interests are not fully aligned* While managers benefit from the size of the funds, because their fees are a percentage of fund assets, investors benefit from their realized return, the growth of the fund's investments after expenses have been deducted. In order to respond to these concerns, the SEC imposed several limitations on the assessment of 12b-1 fees. The first is that 12b-1 fees are only permitted if approved by the fund's board of directors and the majority of the board is independent of the management company. The board of directors is required to regularly re-evaluate the benefits to investors of the imposition of 12b-1 fee. A second limitation is that 12b-1 fees are capped at a certain amount.

As of March 2007, roughly 70 percent of fund classes of mutual funds registered in the United States charged a 12b-1 fee. In 2006, according to the Investment Company Institute, funds collectively paid nearly $11 billion on 12b-1 fees in 2005. Currently, 12b-1 plans are used in all sorts of funds, not merely those which are new and growing.

CHAPTER REVIEW QUESTIONS

Answers to Chapter Review Questions are in the Appendix.

---

34. Michael R. Rosella and Domenick Pugliese, "Rule 12b-1: A Look at Past, Present and Future" *Journal of Investment Compliance* Vol. 8 No. 2 (2007): 10.

35. Ibid, 9–10.

1. Which of the following statements regarding twisting and replacement of life insurance policies is correct?

    (A) Twisting is legal.
    (B) Replacement is illegal.
    (C) Twisting is illegal.
    (D) Twisting is confined to internal policy transfers.

2. Illustrations should be described as

    (A) binding legal documents prepared by state insurance departments
    (B) nonbinding legal documents prepared by state insurance departments
    (C) ledger sheets of guaranteed numbers prepared by an insurance company
    (D) ledger sheet of guaranteed and nonguaranteed figures prepared by an insurance company

3. Rebating is legal in which of the following states?

    (A) Colorado and Florida
    (B) Connecticut and Florida
    (C) California and Florida
    (D) Colorado and Connecticut

4. Which of the following statements best describes the text's definition of rebating?

    (A) Rebating is the process of reducing the premium from a secondary policy in order to credit another competing policy.
    (B) Rebating involves reducing the premium or giving some other valuable consideration, not specified in the policy, to the buyer as an inducement to purchase insurance.
    (C) Rebating involves reducing a premium or giving some other consideration to the writing agent as commission for a pending sale.
    (D) Rebating is the process of giving the consumer added dividends from insurance company assets as compensation for poorly performing policies.

5. Professionals compensated within a fee-only model are compensated in all of the following ways, EXCEPT

    (A) assets under management
    (B) hourly rate
    (C) commission only
    (D) flat fee

6. Which of the following influences the design of compensation models within the financial services industry?

    (A) Financial services products and services are entirely and always tax deductible.

    (B) Financial services professionals both provide advice and sell products and services.

    (C) Financial services products and services are considered a luxury item, only available to the wealthy.

    (D) The best financial services products are imported from overseas.

7. In light of recent compliance concerns, which of the following statements is correct?

    (A) Financial advisors should discontinue the use of all illustrations.

    (B) Financial advisors should discontinue the use of illustrations that contain nonguaranteed values.

    (C) Financial advisors should use illustrations with due regard for full disclosure.

    (D) Financial advisors should use illustrations as their primary sales tool.

8. The sale of a life insurance policy issued by an unauthorized insurer may

    (A) present no difficulty to policyowners because unauthorized carriers typically self-insure

    (B) jeopardize policyowners because state guaranty funds typically cover losses only of admitted carriers

    (C) be permitted in a jurisdiction in which neither the agent nor the insured maintains legal contacts

    (D) add to unauthorized carrier costs by forcing carriers to contribute to multistate guaranty fund compacts

READ THE FOLLOWING DIRECTIONS BEFORE CONTINUING

The questions below differ from the preceding questions in that they all contain the word EXCEPT. So you understand fully the basis used in selecting each answer, be sure to read each question carefully.

9. All of the following are "other marketplace practice issues in today's selling environment" that require careful conduct EXCEPT

   (A) product identification
   (B) company ratings
   (C) guaranty fund advertising
   (D) unauthorized practice of law

10. Each of the following circumstances that involves an existing life insurance policy or contract constitutes a replacement EXCEPT

   (A) when a policy is lapsed, forfeited, surrendered or partially surrendered
   (B) when a policy is converted to reduced paid-up insurance
   (C) when a policy is reissued with any reduction in cash value
   (D) when a policy is converted from term insurance to whole life insurance

APPENDIX A: ANSWER KEY TO QUESTIONS

Chapter 1	
Question Number	**Answer**
1	A
2	B
3	B
4	C
5	B
6	A
7	B
8	B
9	C
10	C

Chapter 2 is an exercise and has no questions.

Chapter 3	
Question Number	**Answer**
1	A
2	B
3	D
4	D
5	B
6	A
7	C
8	B
9	D
10	D

Chapter 4	
Question Number	**Answers**

1	D
2	B
3	A
4	B
5	A
6	B
7	D
8	D
9	C
10	C

Chapter 5

Question Number	Answer
1	B
2	D
3	C
4	A
5	C
6	C
7	A
8	C
9	C
10	B

Chapter 6

Question Number	Answer
1	A
2	D
3	D
4	D
5	B
6	A
7	A

8	B
9	B
10	D

Chapter 7	
Question Number	**Answer**
1	D
2	D
3	C
4	C
5	C
6	D
7	C
8	C
9	D
10	D

Chapter 8	
Question Number	**Answer**
1	C
2	D
3	C
4	B
5	C
6	B
7	C
8	B
9	B
10	D

"As an LUTC Fellow, I recognize that the designation carries with it certain duties and responsibilities. And so, guided by the precepts of the Code of Ethics of the National Association of Life Underwriters, I reaffirm that I believe it to be my responsibility:

- To hold my profession in high esteem and strive to enhance its prestige
- To fulfill the needs of my clients to the best of my ability
- To maintain my clients' confidences
- To render exemplary service to my clients and their beneficiaries
- To adhere to professional standards of conduct in helping my clients to protect insurable obligations and attain their financial security objectives
- To present accurately and honestly all facts essential to my clients' decisions
- To perfect my skills and increase my knowledge through continuing education
- To conduct my business in such a way that my example might help raise the professional standard of life underwriting
- To keep informed with respect to applicable laws and regulations and to observe them in the practice of my profession
- To cooperate with others whose services are constructively related to meeting the needs of my clients."

The Professional Pledge

"In all my professional relationships, I pledge myself to the following rule of ethical conduct: I shall, in light of all conditions surrounding those I serve, which I shall make every conscientious effort to ascertain and understand, render that service which, in the same circumstances, I would apply to myself."

The Canons

I. Conduct yourself at all times with honor and dignity.

II. Avoid practices that would bring dishonor upon your profession or The American College.

III. Publicize your achievements in ways that enhance the integrity of your profession.

IV. Continue your studies throughout your working life so as to maintain a high level of professional competence.

V. Do your utmost to attain a distinguished record of professional service.

VI. Support the established institutions and organizations concerned with the integrity of your profession.

VII. Participate in building your profession by encouraging and providing appropriate assistance to qualified persons pursuing professional studies.

VIII. Comply with all laws and regulations, particularly as they relate to professional and business activities.

APPENDIX D: REFERENCE SITES FOR OTHER CODES

NAIFA Code of Ethics:
http://www.naifa.org/about/ethics.cfm

Society of Financial Service Professionals:
http://www.financialpro.org/about/CodeOfProfResp.cfm

Million Dollar Round Table Code of Ethics:
http://www.mdrt.org/membership/CodeofEthics.asp

Certified Financial Planner Standards of Professional Conduct:
http://www.cfp.net/Learn/Ethics.asp

American Council of Life Insurers:
http://www.pueblo.gsa.gov/acli/

The Alumni Association is the premier gathering place for educated professionals

Lifelong Learning

- *Game-Changer*: Gain practice-strengthening insights from top thought leaders on monthly CE webcasts
- *Knowledge Summit*: Attend career-boosting symposiums and lectures
- *News Feed*: Read breaking news on our website's live industry news feed
- *Learning Center*: Enjoy preferred access to The College's unique Financial Services Library

Industry-Wide Recognition

- Alumni Hall of Fame
- Distinguished Alumni Volunteer Award
- Alumnus/Alumna of the Month
- Promotion of your hard-earned designations

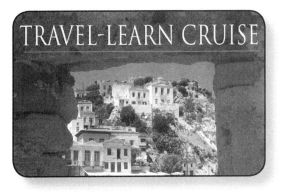

Special Programs

- Embark on special Alumni educational cruises
- Show off your designation with frames, apparel, and jewelry from the Alumni Store
- Take advantage of numerous networking opportunities
- Receive regular newsletters from The College and the Alumni Association

TheAmericanCollege.edu/Alumni

JOIN NOW!

Alumni@TheAmericanCollege.edu
610-526-1477